D0731821

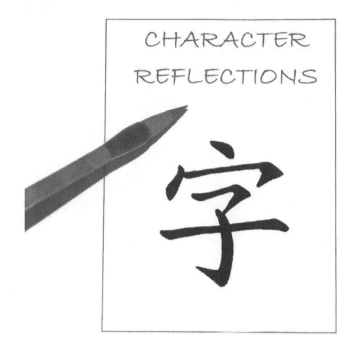

CHARACTER REFLECTIONS

字

Elyn MacInnis

Dedication

To the people around the world who work to understand
and learn from each other
and for my family, all characters in their own right.

Acknowledgements

There are so many people I should acknowledge it leaves my head spinning. On the top of the list is my husband Peter MacInnis, who is the string for my kite. Without you and your kind and gentle help, this book would have never flown. Next are my two daughters, Mika and Charlotte, Charlotte's husband Joshua, and my family, who have given me deep support every step of the way.

Many others have helped – David and Tudy Hill, Jim Capalino and Carlin Vickery, Mark Fretz, and Nan Cobbey were some of the first to see that a book could be born. More recently, fellow Episcopalians Mary Brennan, David Copley, Jane and Titus Butterfield, and Peter Ng and his capable webmasters at Church of Our Savior in New York have provided help and encouragement. Beth Keck and James Baer provided editing assistance. My friends here in China: Yu Ning, our family's first Chinese character teacher; scholars Ming Jie and Ming Yao, Paul and Kristi Wang – calligraphers of extraordinary talent; Feng Cheng of the China Culture Center in Beijing, my dear friend Li Xiao Zhen, and Lily Long, my incredibly talented Chinese language teacher, have all answered endless cultural questions. Wei Jie and friends at the National Radio and Television University have taught me so much about Chinese culture as we worked together on documentaries about Chinese culture and language programs. With deep thanks also to Dick Bodman, Professor and China scholar at St. Olaf's College, for his fine material on the Chinese language which is in the appendix. Deep thanks to Stacie Nakai, who helped me get the book ready for print and was endlessly patient. And a bow to far-flung friends and all the members of Good Shepherd and Trinity Congregations in China, who have shared their thoughts all along the way.

Table of Contents

Chapter One

When I told friends the name of my book was *Character Reflections*, they assumed I was talking about people – the characters who liven up the world with their eccentric and unusual style. China is filled with them, but this is not my topic.

My topic is the Chinese written language – the abc's of Mandarin. But there is a connection between eccentric human characters and the Chinese writing system, in that each uniquely written Chinese character has its own special personality and spirit. The characters in this book have become like friends, and it is my delight to introduce these "characters" to you.

During late winter and early spring of 1999, I began to send out daily spiritual reflections for the members of the Congregation of the Good Shepherd in Beijing and some far-flung friends whom I knew would appreciate some extra spiritual reflections during Lent, the period of forty days before Easter.

In the beginning I just sent a daily quote from a book or respected spiritual writer. Their writing stimulated my own reflections, which I added through the years. Then I turned to meditations on the Chinese characters I was studying, and that struck an even deeper chord both for me, the congregation, and for my friends who received the meditations.   The final version of *Character Reflections* was sent out in 2009 to my new church community in Shanghai, Trinity Congregation, as well as friends, family and interested people around the world.

Why call this book *Character Reflections*? It is not just because it contains "reflections" on the roots of the characters, but because the characters *reflect* a pool of universal truth that is inspiring no matter what background you come from.   The truth in the ancient roots of these Chinese characters will touch your heart, stimulate your mind, and be helpful in the search for wisdom to shape our lives.

Although "reflections" might seem passive, a reflection is actually quite dynamic, changing with perspective and light.   This book is meant to serve as the light energy that helps move your spiritual practice, and transform and enrich your understanding of the world.

Because I am an Episcopal priest, the spirit of Jesus, his Way and spiritual practice described in the gospels is my background.   But there is a larger picture that goes beyond any one religion or culture.   Practicing compassion, love, kindness, forgiveness, understanding, wisdom, patience and joy is spiritually resonant for people of all faiths, and is the place where we will begin to nurture peace in the world and allow ourselves to be enriched by those whose culture is different from our own.   That is why Chinese characters are a good place to begin.

Because Chinese characters were formed thousands of years ago, arising from deep within the Asian cultural tradition and mindset, they bring many delights and surprises to Westerners. I have been enchanted and amazed by where their stories and roots have led me.

I have tried to meet each character with open and simple eyes, and enjoy the places where East meets West. Having a receptive and respectful heart makes it possible to welcome new ideas and celebrate our shared humanity and spiritual practice. It is my hope that this book will be used both by Christians on a spiritual journey, and also by anyone who is interested in the ancient wisdom embodied in Chinese characters and its application to their daily life.

About the author

In 1988 my husband, Peter, our two daughters, Mika and Charlotte, and I settled in Nanjing, the capital of Jiangsu Province.   This was before development fueled the modern high-tech high-rise China we know today.

Of all our family members, Peter felt the most at home in Nanjing, perhaps because he was born in China in 1948 when his parents taught English at Hua Nan Women's College in Fuzhou. His father, Donald, had taken his first trip to

China in 1939, teaching English at a high school that had evacuated to the mountains during the Sino-Japanese War. He later returned to China during World War II serving with the "Flying Tigers" unit of the Army protecting China from Japanese forces. Peter's family moved to Taiwan when he was five.

Although my family did not have deep China roots (I was born in New York City!), I felt curiously at home in Nanjing.   What I remember was the kindness of our friends and co-workers, who gave us great happiness.

We were happy, but life was not easy. The children's school and my husband's office did not have heat in those days, in spite of below freezing temperatures that gripped the city during the coldest part of the winter. Although we had a tiny hot water heater at home, most of Nanjing was coping with no heat or hot water except water that was boiled on coal stoves. My work was based at home, so I could drink eternal cups of hot tea and disappear in a pile of comforters during the winter, except on Mondays, when the electricity in the district was shut down and rerouted for the day to share with other districts.

We rode bikes, bought our vegetables fresh off farmer's tarps at the local "free market," and coped with the black smoke from the coal water heater smokestack outside our living room window that provided an hour of hot water in the evenings. We lived in great abundance compared to our friends and neighbors, some of whom washed their family's laundry in huge tubs of freezing cold water on the sidewalk.

Was it difficult? In some ways.   But no more difficult than for everyone else. In fact, we lived in luxury.   We had the luxury of hiding in bed to watch TV or read or do homework. We had hot water and some heat. We had the luxury of living in a city of wonderfully warm and generous people who taught us how to live through freezing temperatures in the winter and intense heat in the summer.

Since everything was done at a slower pace, I knew I could plan to do one thing in the morning, and one thing in the afternoon. For example, take a trip to the bank. It took at least two hours to get some cash out of our account. But the trip was fascinating because they used a system of hand written and hand stamped account books, and the dimly-lit cavernous hall was a delightful place to rest while the transaction made its way around the bank collecting red stamps on the bankbook and the many pages of forms that accompanied it.

We had front row seats to watch as China grew and developed into the fast paced and modern center of Asia that it has now become. Now, with shining subways and tall high rises, China has cities that rival the best anywhere in the world.

It has been my honor to have served as minister of three congregations in my time in China, at Saint Paul's Church in Nanjing, the Congregation of the Good Shepherd in Beijing, and at Trinity Congregation in Shanghai, all different, and yet each one blessed with thoughtful members with deep compassion and wisdom.

My story has been my own, and at the same time I have been deeply affected by many friends and co-workers of great spiritual depth. Where their lives have intertwined with mine, I have been truly enriched.

It has been my honor to have worked with many leaders and ministers in the China Christian Council churches around China who are some of the finest shepherds I know, and whose congregations are kind, enthusiastic, encouraging, and insightful.

I think of Pastor Wang in Chong Qing who, when the disastrous earthquake occurred in Sichuan in 2008, jumped into a truck with members of her congregation and drove with water, medicine and tents to help the people in the earthquake zone within a few hours after she received the news of the quake. I also think of Pastor Bao, who, along with his work in Bible distribution for the China Christian Council, also works with minority congregations in Yunnan, helping them to find ways to build new church buildings and get training for the local leadership. I think of Rev. Mou at Saint Paul's Church, who gave her own blankets away to the seminary students from the South who, because they came from a warm climate, did not have enough blankets to keep warm at night. And many more pastors too numerous to name here.

It has also been my honor to work with leaders of many NGOs and service projects around China, most notably "Granny" Han Ru Fen of the Peng Cheng Special Education School in Xuzhou, Jiangsu Province, where love and openness to new ideas and methods has given birth to one of the finest Special Education schools in the country. During a recent visit I met one of her many successes, a young man who was asked to leave the public schools because he was too violent. Granny Han agreed to take him at the school for a trial period.

Within three months of his arrival, not only was he no longer violent and in good control of himself, but he also spoke without prompting for the first time in his life. His words to his mother, as she took him home for lunch on her bike, were: "Mama, I have lollipops to share with you." His story is not unusual at Granny Han's school, and many other children have had miraculous growth and development under her capable leadership.

I am also honored to know and work with Peter and Ruth Xu of the Golden Key Center in Beijing, who have been tireless in their efforts to help blind and vision impaired children in extreme poverty areas become integrated into their local classrooms. The first time I traveled with them in the deep mountains north of Xi'an where the villagers still live in caves, I met a twelve year old girl who for years had stood at the door of the local school listening to the lessons until winter cold made it impossible. When the Golden Key team came and trained the principal and teachers in Chinese Braille, making it possible for her to attend class, she courageously joined in and worked hard to catch up. She told me: "I used to feel like I was a completely useless person. But now I can go to school, and I am going to study hard and some day be able to make a contribution to my community."

I am also honored to know and have worked with the amazing crew at the Springbud Foundation in Beijing, who have arranged for young girls to attend school during the years before tuition-free education was available, and who now dedicate themselves to improving the school environments of children in poor districts all over China.

And it has been a special honor to work with the staff at the Amity Foundation, which supports dozens of projects all over China with integrity, heart, and compassion. It was through the Amity Foundation, China's first NGO, that I first met so many of the incredible leaders of NGOs and service projects all around China, including Granny Han, Peter and Ruth Xu and more. I am greatly indebted to them for their deep wisdom, insight, and compassion.

About Chinese characters

When I began to learn characters, my teacher at the time told me, "Just memorize them." I was overwhelmed. To be considered literate, you must memorize some 3,000 characters.

Our twenty-six English letters all come with sound(s) and if you put them together you can usually understand how to pronounce a word. Looking them up in the dictionary is a simple procedure. But characters? I hardly knew where to begin. Each one looked like someone had taken a plate of spaghetti and dumped it on the table!

I later learned there are parts used to construct Chinese characters, and these are very useful in helping to remember the meanings.

Chinese characters are constructed in several ways, but they can be composed of:

❖ <u>parts that are **phonetic**</u> that indicate the sound.

❖ <u>parts with meaning or indicating a category of meaning</u>. These are called **radicals**, like the three dots of water 氵 which often appear on the left side of a character usually indicating something liquid.

❖ <u>parts that are ideographs</u>, or **picture** characters, like the character for mouth, 口 which is just a square box, or the character for person, 人 which looks like someone on a walk.

Ninety percent of modern Chinese characters are made up of a **radical** (like the water drops, indicating category of meaning) and a **phonetic**, which indicates pronunciation. But phonetics can also add to the meaning of the character, and are not just simply a sound.

For a more detailed and thorough discussion of Chinese characters, please see the appendix. Chinese character scholars please note: I am not claiming any new scholarly insight or knowledge that is not already present in dictionaries or texts. I am merely presenting my own personal thoughts and insights that have come to me upon learning the ancient roots of the characters.

In the following chapters, each character's parts will be explained first, followed by stories, reflections and quotes.   The order of the characters has no particular thread, but each one stands on its own. So please feel free to move throughout the book and enjoy them as you are drawn to them in whatever order feels right to you.

This introduction ends perfectly with a quick peek at the characters used for the word "to begin"

Kai   Shi
To Begin

On the Left : Kai means doors, evenly opened.

On the Right: Shi is a character made of two parts,

a woman on the left hand side,

with the representation of joy on the right.

Indeed, this is how this book began.

Stop – Ting

Left side: A person

Right side: A pavilion

Put together, a person resting against a pavilion carries the meaning of "stop".   No doubt the person is sitting in the shade resting from his or her work!

There is a story from China about stopping:

A person was standing by the road when a horse and rider came galloping by raising clouds of dust. The person at the side of the road, thinking that something important must be happening, called out to the rider, "Hey! Where are you going?"

The rider called back loudly, "I don't know! Ask my horse!"

There are many horses to ride:

The horses of <u>Habits</u>, especially being overly busy. We run around frantically each day – for work, for school, to shop, run errands, play sports, workout, run, jog, clean the house, yard, car, take the dogs for a walk, do laundry, or sit in front of the TV exhausted.

The horses of <u>Emotions</u>, like anger, worry, or depression, hate, jealousy or greed. We can miss the delight of simply being alive by winding ourselves up with negative emotions.

Or we may be riding the horses of <u>Desires and Hunger</u> for what we don't have, or think we need. I can remember when our children were small being overwhelmed with the desire for our own house. It is easy to think that we must have a certain brand of something, a certain way of living, a longer vacation or a fancier pet.

This character reminds us to stop the horse and reassess what we are doing. But to stop the horse, we first need to become aware of what it is we should stop and also become aware of our state of mind so we can keep it from taking us over.

Stopping our bodies is easier than stopping our minds. The character shows a person leaning their body against the side of a pavilion. The real challenge is to take the time to stop our mind and give it a rest.

Someone with a mathematical bent has added up all the time average Americans spend sitting at stoplights during their lives: about six months. Most people anxiously await the turn of the light to green. We scheme about how we will pull in front of some other car so we can be first, or gnash our teeth about being late. But in these stopped moments we can use our minds to take a break. We can make the choice to think about something else.

The possibilities are delightful! Sending love to someone, enjoying the green leaves on the trees, contemplating the subtlety of the winter landscape, savoring the cup of tea or coffee you just sipped, saying a prayer of thanks for the good things happening in your life, or even just breathing.

I haven't seen figures for how many minutes we use brushing our teeth, or boiling water for a cup of tea or coffee, but we really do have many opportunities to "stop" our constant worry or mind chatter and consciously create how we want to feel in our life. If that seems like a lot, at a stoplight you can simply hum your favorite song. It doesn't have to be complicated. Stopping provides us with the time and potential to choose how we want to feel while we go about our daily tasks.

Happiness – Yu Kuai

Left side: heart	Left side: heart
Right side: when boating	Right side: hand holding something

Of the many words for happiness in Chinese, this one is most fanciful. The second character, kuai, is a phonetic word and just supports the first. But the first character caught my eye right away because it is composed of a heart (left) gone boating (right), describing a joyful state of happiness.

   **A note about the representations for the heart. The actual character representing the heart is horizontal and appears in other characters having to do with feelings and matters of the heart. But there is also a form that appears in a vertical form. It looks like this:

This form of the "heart" is on the left side of both characters in *yu kuai*: 愉快. Standing up it looks much less like a heart, but that is its meaning.

When I was a child I lived in an apartment that overlooked the Hudson River. What a blessing the river was to me. My heart could go boating. I could watch it for hours, viewing the progress of big barges that were being pushed up-river by round red tugboats with the huge tassel of thick ropes that protects the front of the boat from harm. Huge container ships docked on the other side of the river in New Jersey, and I could watch endless construction of fancy high-rises. Every night we had lovely sunsets so beautiful they would leave me breathless – glorious reds, fluorescent pinks, burnished gold. Evening would bring its own peace, and in the winter when the trees had lost their leaves I could watch the tiny lights of cars on the Hudson River Parkway or boats out in the night, which gave me a wonderful cozy feeling to be in my own little warm room.

You may feel like a boat captain on the river. Maybe like the boat? Maybe you feel more like you are watching the river from the window. All of these are part of our journey – but when we can capture that free flowing feeling of our heart joyfully streaming along in the flow of life, we have entered a true state of happiness.

Here are two prayers of Celtic origin to bring you happiness on your journey.

Be you a bright flame before me.
Be you a smooth way below me.
Be you a guiding star above me.
Be you a watchful eye behind me.
This day, this night, forever.
~ **Traditional Celtic Prayer**

The Lord be with you as you go.
Bless you in your coming.
The presence be with your journey.
Bless your road as it unwinds.
~ **attributed to Saint Columba, Ireland, 521-597**

Forget – Wang

Top: to escape

Bottom: heart

As is true for so many Chinese words about important concepts, the heart is often there, this time at the bottom of the character. The top part means "to escape." If something has escaped from your heart, it is forgotten.

Recently I read an article about a famous children's book author from China named Bing Xin. She died in 1999 at the age of 99, leaving behind a legacy of dozens of beloved children's books and stories. She chose topics about the family and nature, and her stories have been in Chinese elementary school textbooks for generations. My daughters read her story about a tangerine lantern when they were in elementary school in Nanjing. Her stories were encouraging. She wrote, "Walking on the long road of life, with love on the right and sympathy on the left, is just like blossoming and seeding. Travelers on such a scented journey will neither feel pain when stepping on brambles nor taste grief when shedding tears."

As with all authors during the Cultural Revolution, things were not easy. She stopped writing for years until 1980, when she picked up her pen again and began to write stories to expose or expound on social problems such as reform in rural areas, education for women and children, and the treatment given to intellectuals. Her soft language changed, and she was known for being very direct, pointed, and fearless. Bing Xin was once asked by her daughter why she was restarting her career in her eighties. She answered, "Forget whatever should be forgotten, so you can remember what should be remembered."

It is a blessing to have things "escape" from your heart. When we put aside old hurts and forget the things that should be put aside and forgotten, we make room for a whole new direction. That direction is not clouded by our past, but can be led by those things that should be remembered, like the importance of kindness, support, encouragement, and humor in your relationships with others.

Remember your humanity and forget the rest.
~ **Albert Einstein 1879 – 1955, from the "Russell – Einstein Manifesto"**

Recompense injury with justice, and recompense kindness with kindness.
~ **Confucius 551 – 479 BCE, Analects Chapter 14**

Forget the former things;
    do not dwell on the past.
See, I am doing a new thing!
Now it springs up; do you not perceive it?
I am making a way in the desert
    and streams in the wasteland.
~ **Isaiah 43:18-19, 6th Century BCE,**

Finish each day and be done with it. You have done what you could. Some blunders and absurdities no doubt crept in; forget them as soon as you can. Tomorrow is a new day; begin it well and serenely and with too high a spirit to be encumbered with your old nonsense.
~ **Ralph Waldo Emerson (1803 – 1882) from a letter to his daughter who was away at school**

To Arrive - Lin

Left side: a person prostrating on the ground,
a sign of respect in China.
Right side: chosen for its phonetic sound,
not its meaning.

How interesting it is that the Chinese character for "arrive" shows the aspect of respect and devotion.

Spring arrives whether we want it or not – although if you live in a cold climate, spring is very welcome. We don't do anything to bring about the arrival of spring. We might be anxious for it, long for it, pray for it, but spring comes on its own. In Shanghai, we had a sneak preview of spring one February which was so delicious that it left everyone breathless for more warm weather. But then winter closed in again, and we were back to dreary cold and piercing wet air that made us anxious to crawl into our beds at night with the heater-blanket turned on high.

I can remember walking with a scholar friend along a Beijing canal in the freezing cold weather of late January just after Chinese New Year. It wasn't a little cold – it was bitter cold. And I was a bit surprised when he asked if I could feel spring in the air. I hadn't thought about it, but it was there. Even though it was still cold, the seasons had turned the corner, and there was something soft about the wind. Spring had arrived even though the temperature was hovering below freezing.

When paired with the character for "time," "arrive" morphs into the word for "temporary." It is also used in the phrase for welcoming you to a store or a restaurant, roughly translated as "Welcoming (Your) Bright Arrival!" I should have said that to the universe on that cold day I felt spring in the air walking along the canal in Beijing.

There is real wisdom in using the same word for "temporary" as for "arrival". Change is profound. We are in a state of constant change, and that is something worthy of devotion. The lime tree grows and makes limes. We grow and change too, in all aspects. If we were frozen like a person sitting in the snow and never changed, we could never experience the vibrancy and new life of spring. Each arrival is really a temporary spot for changes that will bring about our future. Winter evolves into Spring.

You may have heard of Julian of Norwich (1342 - 1416), who is associated with the mystical tradition of Christianity. During her time the world was faced with many difficult situations: the plague, the Hundred Year's War, and a crisis in church authority. So many things were changing around her, like great tides and waves, as it is in our time.

Julian lived in a cell as a hermit in Norwich, England. She wasn't cut off completely from the world, however. There were two windows in her cell. From one window, which looked out at the altar of the church, she would receive communion, and through the other window, which opened to the outside, she received meals and give spiritual advice to the people who came to her for wisdom in the changing times in which they lived.

During a serious illness that brought her near death, Julian had revelations of Christ's passion, after which she recovered from her illness completely. In the deep winter of her life, the breeze of spring arrived. She may have thought that she would die, but change does not always bring what we expect. After this experience her idea of the cross changed. To her the cross was not something scary or sad, but was "a kind of consolation," which she considered a sign of Christ's "friendliness" and "courtesy." She had visual revelations of Christ's bleeding head, but in her spiritual eye what she saw was God's love and goodness. The cold breeze of change was temporary and had in the end brought her new spiritual warmth.

※ ☀ ☀

As Julian of Norwich tells us, "In falling and rising again we are held in that same precious love." Only to the extent that we let go into change can we live in harmony with those around us and with our own true nature. No matter what situation, awakening requires trust; trust in the greater cycles of life, trust that something new will eventually be born, trust that whatever is, is perfect. Wise letting go is not a detached removal from life. It is the heart's embrace of life itself, a willing opening to the full reality of the present.

~ **From On Julian of Norwich, by Jack Kornfield**

Rest – Xiu Xi

Left: person	Top: self
Right: tree	Bottom: heart

Xiu xi, pronounced "shoe-she," also means "to rest" and is related to the idea of "stopping". The first character has someone leaning against a tree. Xi, on the right, has the character for "self," a finger pointing to one's nose, on the top, with the heart on the bottom.

In Western countries, when you point to yourself, you point to your heart or the middle of your chest.

Say, "Who, me?" Just point to yourself to try it out.

In Asian countries, you point to your nose instead.

So are we pointing to our chests, and to our noses, or is it that we are pointing to our hearts (in our chest) and our minds (inside our heads)?

In the West we talk about our *minds* and what our *mind* is thinking. For Westerners, the brain is the "mind". In Asia, the "mind" is embodied in the heart. You can see this in the Chinese word for psychology: 心理学 (literal translation: heart-inside-study of) the study of the heart. The truth about resting is embodied in this ancient character. To truly rest, we need not just rest our mind, but also our hearts.

There is a secret to resting. If we truly rest our physical self and refrain from action, our outer motion stops, and then our inner motion, our thoughts, become more noticeable. When we learn how to stop our thoughts from racing around, we reach a place of real rest. This is why it is so important to learn meditation.

Anyone who has tried to meditate and "let go of all thoughts" knows about how busy the mind gets when you quiet the body. The character *Xi* is one of the characters used in the word for *breathing*. Paying attention to the breath is one of the most basic forms of contemplation and meditation, and gives both the brain and heart a chance to rest and relax. This is one of the secrets of true rest.

When we come to a point of rest in our own being, we encounter a world where all things are at rest, and then a tree becomes a mystery, a cloud becomes a revelation, and each person we meet a cosmos whose riches we can only glimpse.

~ Dag Hammarskjöld, 1905-61, Second Secretary General of the United Nations

Come to me, all you who are weary and burdened, and I will give you rest. Take my yoke upon you and learn from me, for I am gentle and humble in heart, and you will find rest for your souls.

~ Matt 11:28-29

Knowledge - Zhi Shi

Left: a man shooting an arrow	Left: words
Right: a mouth	Middle: sound
	Right: a lance

Look first at the character on the left. It is made up of two parts: a man shooting an arrow standing next to a mouth on the right. You can see that someone who has knowledge "can get the point." They hear what the mouth is saying, and can focus on what is important, the point.

The character on the right contains three parts – words, sound and a lance. This character carries the same idea. The lance pierces through the words to the inner meaning.

Here is a conundrum:

The intellect is essential for someone aspiring to a spiritual path. Without intellectual study, people can end up being purely superstitious. In intellectual contemplation we look at details and analyze, make categories and memorize. We look at doctrines, at history, theology, and analyze parables and myth.

Some things can be understood using our brains and our intellect, but there is other knowledge that can only be truly grasped from our hearts.

Spiritual contemplation is like this. When we do spiritual practice, there are no details, analysis, or things to memorize, but there is pure action from the heart of our being. Spiritual life requires real involvement in life, not just study.   Love, compassion, understanding, forgiveness – these are spiritual actions, not intellectual points.   Balancing the intellectual and the spiritual is always a challenge.   If you feel most comfortable with the intellectual, focusing on the spiritual will be what brings you growth. If you feel more comfortable in the active spiritual side of life, then focusing yourself in intellectual pursuit will bring you new development.

Leave – Li Bie

Left: ox or water buffalo	Left: represents idea of "separately"
Right: bird	Right: knife

The word for "leave" or "depart" is made up of two characters.

The character Li, on the left, depicts an ox or water buffalo and a bird. Birds fly off quickly when they leave. The ox is there because it is the animal the famous philosopher Laozi rode as he departed from China after writing his famous classic "Dao De Jing" (Tao Te Ching).

Leaving is something we don't take much notice of in the West. We go to the airport by ourselves, and when we say good-bye to someone they do not accompany us to the street, but say good-bye and shut the door. In China it is different - leaving is a time for friends to express their friendship and deepen their relationship. There are thousands of famous and beloved poems about parting and arriving, like this one:

Parting at a Wine Shop in Nanjing

A wind, bringing willow-cotton*, sweetens the shop,
And a girl from Wu, pouring wine, urges me to share it

With my comrades of the city who are here to see me off;

And as each of them drains his cup, I say to him in parting,

Oh, go and ask this river running to the east

If it can travel farther than a friend's love!

~ Li Bai, China's most famous poet, 701- 762

*Note: In China there are many cottonwood trees, and in the spring it looks like it is snowing from all the fluffy white "cotton" with seeds attached -- a bit like the dandelion -- that floats in the air as the tree sends out its many seeds. The Chinese call the cottonwood a "willow" because it grows at the edge of streams like the weeping willow. It is in the Poplar family of fast growing trees, and is the state tree of Nebraska.

I remember when we just arrived in China how confused I was when our good friends wanted to accompany our family to the airport when we went on one of our periodic trips out of the country. I would have to expend no small effort to convince them that it wasn't necessary. For me, it felt like an added burden.   But I later realized that for them it indicated how they felt about our family and was a sign of our deep relationship.   They were not even thinking about the time they would have to spend going to the airport to see us off when we were leaving. They were just honoring our friendship.

The importance of leaving and going partway with someone on their journey brings up another issue. In the United States, our main focus is our tasks at hand – how to get the job done quicker and more efficiently, or even just how to get as many chores done as possible in one day.   We see a trip to the airport as just another task, and feel badly if we "interfere" with someone else's work or time, so we would never want someone to come with us to the airport.

In the East, the focus has always been on developing harmonious relationships, not on task, and that is why our Chinese friends wanted to go to the airport with us -- to show they cared for us and that our relationship was significant to them.

The concept of focusing on relationship instead of task made me think about the story of Mary and Martha, Jesus' female disciples. Jesus went to

Martha's house where she was immediately distracted by all the tasks and preparations she felt necessary for this great teacher and his disciples. In contrast, Mary, her sister, sat down at Jesus' feet and focused on what he was saying. I suspect he was not just chatting, but teaching. When Martha scolded Mary and told Jesus that Mary should help with the work, he instead recognized Mary for staying with the group and choosing to listen to his teaching. They don't say what happened next. I hope Martha sat down and listened to his teaching too! And perhaps they all helped with dinner later on. It isn't clear. But in the end, the task – making dinner – never made it into the story. But the story of deep relationship did. In the choice between task and relationship, relationship won.

In the US, two thousand years later, we have elevated our work and tasks to an even higher position than ever before. Tasks consume us. Our jobs are the main point of our lives; we work more hours than ever before. There is almost no time for developing and nurturing relationships. Our children are loaded down with school, homework, study, and after school activities and lessons, and maybe a few hours of television to keep them busy while we are busy. If a modern Jesus came to a modern Martha's house, she probably wouldn't even be at home – she would still be at work.

In Asia, relationship is put before task most of the time. How can you accomplish a task well if you don't have a good relationship? And if you consider the story of Mary and Martha, we are pointed in this direction: to consider and give more weight to our relationships and our spiritual development in community.

One of my favorite task versus relationship stories is about an American English teacher in China. One weekend he planned to go with a group of his Chinese students to a neighboring town of historical note. They were to visit the town, review its history, and have a picnic there. When they got to the railway station, they could see the train down on the tracks steaming and making the last call for travelers. They raced down the corridors and long flight of stairs huffing and puffing, leapt on the train, and congratulated each other as they made their way to their seats. As they settled in and the conductor came around to collect their tickets, they realized that they had hopped on the wrong train, and that it was going in the opposite direction! The teacher was extremely upset and agitated but the students gradually calmed him down. The students brightly suggested that they could just get off at first stop and have their picnic there. After all, they told him, what was important was to have a happy time with each other and a picnic together in the spring sunshine.

Whether we are leaving or arriving, and wherever we may find ourselves, it is the way we relate to those around us that matters most.

God, Spirit - Shen

Left: an omen or sign from heaven.

Right: a phonetic character, which also adds to the meaning.

If you look carefully, you can see two hands holding a body, which is the straight line in the middle. The hands are the forward facing "E" on the left of the center line, and the opposite, reversed "E" on the right side of the center line. This character carries the meaning of "spirit".

At our home in Providence, RI, we often have windy days in the spring and fall, with gusts up to 40 or 50 miles per hour. You can't see the wind. You might be able to see the dust in the wind or a plastic bag flying in the wind, but you can't see the wind itself. However, you can feel it. There are other important things in the world that we can't see but can feel.

Spirit is like the wind. Sometimes you can see it, but mostly it is felt like the wind, not seen in physical form.

Jesus compared the wind to God's spirit. "The wind blows wherever it pleases. You hear its sound, but you cannot tell where it comes from or where it is going. So it is with everyone born of the Spirit." This is true. The material world is easy to grasp, but the spiritual is not like a physical item which you can show someone. It is present like the wind – giving us "lift" and "momentum", moving us higher than living for ourselves alone and deeper into awareness and understanding for everyone and everything.

This is what Jesus meant by our "second birth" – not from the body, but from the spirit, when our perceptions change and we see the divine presence in the world, which like the wind is invisible, but can be perceived if your eyes are attuned to it.

I know that small children often think the trees make the wind by waving their branches. I love that idea. Last year I talked to a group of small children about this idea. One incredibly bright-eyed boy looked at me with intense earnestness. "The Wind is…. Invisible!" he chortled. Everyone there agreed. So began a discussion of what we can't see. They enjoyed the idea of not being able to see themselves growing, or the stars in the daytime. And then we talked about love. Can you see love? Who loves you? They were so intense. Mom, Dad, Grandpa or Grandma, friends, teachers, dogs, cats, pet bird – one child even said Santa! Love comes in so many ways: in the form of hugs, kisses, encouragement, time spent together, giving and receiving, helping and caring, but also in an intangible form like the wind, a breeze that fills and nourishes the heart with gladness.

We stopped there. That is the mystery of Love.

I thought you might enjoy this poem from Rumi, the great Persian spiritual master who lived in the 1200s and wrote some of the finest spiritual poetry the world has ever known.

We are as the flute, and the music in us is from thee;
   we are as the mountain and the echo in us is from thee.
We are as pieces of chess engaged in victory and defeat:
   our victory and defeat is from thee, O thou whose
   qualities are comely!
Who are we, O Thou soul of our souls,
   that we should remain in being beside thee?
We and our existences are really non-existence;
   thou art the absolute Being which manifests
   the perishable.

We all are lions, but lions on a banner:
  because of the wind they are rushing onward
  from moment to moment.
Their onward rush is visible, and the wind is unseen:
  may that which is unseen not fail from us!
Our wind whereby we are moved and our being are of
    thy gift;
  our whole existence is from thy bringing into being.
~ Rumi, Persian mystic, 1207-1273, from the Masnavi, Book I, 599-607

He who dwells in the shelter of the Most High
  will abide in the shadow of the Almighty.
~ Psalm 91

My real dwelling
Has no pillars
And no roof either
So rain cannot soak it
And wind cannot blow it down.

Every day priests minutely examine the scriptures
And endlessly chant complicated sutras.
Before doing that, though, they should learn
How to read the love letters
Sent by the wind and rain, the snow and moon.
~Ikkyu, Japanese Zen master and poet, 1400s.

Mystical, Mystery - Shen Qi

Left: omen or sign from heaven.	Top: person standing with their arms wide apart
Right: phonetic character with 2 hands holding a body.	Bottom: person, the box representing their mouth, exhaling in awe and wonder

Shen, the character on the left, means God and also spirit.   When combined with the character *Qi*, which means unusual, it creates a compound word, *Shen-qi*, which means Mystical or Mysterious.

How wonderful it is that we can experience awe. I recently watched in awe as the shadow of the sun made its way across the moon in a lunar eclipse, connecting me with the enormity and complexity of the cosmos. And I listened in awe to some children as they talked about the people they loved and how they knew it. I am so glad that every question doesn't necessarily have an answer. Our understanding and grasp of the world is so limited. We are surrounded with mystery. To open our hearts wide and accept the mystery of our existence is spiritual nourishment for our deepest being.

Jesus talks about seeds sprouting, growing and flourishing, first the blade, then the ear, then full grain. No one arranges it. Divine grace can sprout and burst into our awareness suddenly, like a seed breaking open. It is a mystery beyond comprehension. And if we are aware of that grace and nourish it, it ripens into seeds of compassion, gratitude, and wisdom. When we are aware, we can skate on the surface of mystery and sometimes fall in, becoming immersed in the nurturing water of divine grace and love.

God is not what you imagine or what you think you understand. If you understand you have failed.
~ **Saint Augustine, Church Father, philosopher, and theologian (354 – 430)**

What is indispensable is for us to recognize that this world is not self-evident. The visible is nothing more than a path to revealing the invisible — light serving to disclose the hidden light of light itself.
~ **Rabbi Nilton Bonder, Brazilian author of <u>Yiddishe Kop</u>**

The most beautiful and deepest experience a man can have is the sense of the mysterious. It is the underlying principle of religion as well as all serious endeavour in art and science. He who never had this experience seems to me, if not dead, then at least blind. To sense that behind anything that can be experienced there is a something that our mind cannot grasp and whose beauty and sublimity reaches us only indirectly and as a feeble reflection, this is religiousness. In this sense I am religious. To me it suffices to wonder at these secrets and to attempt humbly to grasp with my mind a mere image of the lofty structure of all that there is.
~ **Albert Einstein, in The World As I See It (1949)**

Perseverance – Ren

Top – knife

Bottom – heart

This character speaks for itself. It is the character for knife held directly over the heart.

    I can remember the first time I was surprised by the word "perseverance." I was huddled over a Chinese manuscript writing a description of the different tunes performed by the Nanjing Folk Music Orchestra. The translator's English had some delightful moments, but basically I could not understand her. One evening I floated right up out of my chair to where the translator was standing at the side of the stage and found myself asking if I couldn't help her create a simple English script that she could memorize for their performance.

    I translated the program with the help of my daughters' Chinese teacher and my music teacher. We labored over the descriptions, and finally came to my favorite piece, "Three Varieties of Plum Blossom." The Plum tree is revered all over Asia. I once went to a garden in Tokyo that was famous for its plum trees just as the rich purple buds began to open. So many visitors were there, and the park was packed with older people in dark colored kimonos, business men in suits, and mothers with school children in tow like strings of ducklings. We all meandered through the tiny park, cheek by jowl, peering at the flowers, taking close ups of the blooms with our cameras, and arranging group photos posed with the blossoming trees. It was a beautiful sight – but why all the fuss over plum blossoms?

For some reason, the translator had no trouble with the translation of the Plum Blossom melody description. She said, in perfectly clear English, "The Plum blossom is the symbol for Nanjing. It is Nanjing's City Flower. It means…" She halted and looked me straight in the eye… "perseverance." Her eyes were penetrating like deep black pools. I think I fell into them. From the intensity of her look it was clear there was profound meaning. Perseverance?

She explained to me that the plum tree blooms first of all the spring trees, enduring snow, freezing temperatures, and all kinds of hardship. Now it became clear. Whoever chose the Plum blossom as the city flower for Nanjing picked it in truthfulness – of all the cities in China, it has endured more difficulties than most. As the capital city of four dynasties and two kingdoms, it was built and destroyed, sometimes back to farmland, quite a few times. A center for turbulence in China, in the past 150 years alone Nanjing persevered and endured the slaughter of incredible numbers of its people – when the "Taiping Heavenly Kingdom" came to an end in the late 1800s with the massacre and suicide of some 100,000 people. During the civil war in China in the 1920's 100,000 more citizens lost their lives, and also during the war with Japan in the 30's, during which 300,000 men, women and children died. Persevering and enduring with grace and beauty in spite of terrible times – this is the character of Nanjing and its people. For the future, we must picture peace prevailing for these sturdy people.

If you go outside Nanjing to the Purple Mountains there is a hillside park covered in a haze of plum trees in the early spring where the people of Nanjing go for outings. The park draws incredible crowds, so numerous that the trees can disappear in the swarms of Nanjingers. Early in my time in China I disliked visiting the park when there were such crowds, but I grew a different feeling about it once I understood the symbol and its meaning. The Plum trees dance their purple dance of enduring perseverance in the spring, and the people of Nanjing were celebrating with them.

Warm rain and soft breeze by turns
Have just broken
And driven away the chill.
Moist as the pussy willows,
Light as the plum blossoms,
Already I feel the heart of Spring vibrating.

~ Li Qing Zhao, Song Dynasty Poet of the 1100s who lived in Nanjing when her husband was Mayor

Gratitude and Thanks – Xie

Left: Word – a mouth on the bottom with vapors (words) coming out and up.
Center and Right: a body in the center, originally paired with the character for arrow on the right. Put together, they carry the meaning of to shoot, or an arrow being shot.

Put two of these characters together and you make the word "*Xie xie*," which means "thank you."

One of my favorite feelings is gratitude. Sometimes, what appears to be a catastrophe turns out to be a blessing, like the time my car ran out of gas on the New York Thruway when I was in college.

A car saw us standing by the road and stopped. Dale, the friend I was driving home with, and I had a glimmer of hope. Maybe this person would help us? The car stopping was a big black mobster-style Oldsmobile. When the driver got out, we were shocked to see our "savior" wearing a black overcoat, fedora hat, dark sunglasses, and black leather gloves. He walked over to our car with a stiff-legged gait. Could he be anyone else but a mobster? He certainly looked like a traditional mobster. Adding to that impression, as he pulled a container of gasoline out of his car trunk, I noticed that one of his hands was missing and there was a hook instead! I am telling the 100% unvarnished truth. But he stayed to make sure we could start the car, and followed us to be certain we had enough gas to get off the Thruway safely.

Can you imagine that?   We were so grateful. As we thanked him for his help, he said that he just hoped that someone would do the same for his daughter if she were stranded on the side of the highway. I remain in a cloud of perpetual gratitude for this kind person and his loving heart.

Gratitude is a pointer, much like the arrow that was put into the character. Gratitude is pointing to a blessing. We are grateful FOR something, and we have chosen to see it as a blessing. This choice is also critical.

When our family first arrived in Nanjing in 1988, no one in town had heat. No one in the countryside had heat either! Nor did many workplaces, including Peter's, or schools, including the one my two daughters attended. In February, often around Valentine's Day, the temperatures would plunge below freezing, and in the evening, local families would quickly eat dinner, wash up, and then all pile into bed together and watch television or do homework under the covers. I was constantly awash with gratitude for the blessing of the little heaters we had in our living room that kept our house hovering around 50 degrees Fahrenheit.   There are at least two ways to look at it – some might say we suffered. I like to think that we were really blessed to have some heat. I am happy to say that most Nanjingers now have some form of heat that will at least take the edge off the deep cold of winter.

Whether we feel gratitude or are bitter depends on a choice we make – not the situation we find ourselves in. We often do not have control over what happens in our lives, which we notice especially when we have difficulties, like a car accident or illness. But we do have control over how we decide to process what has happened, how we integrate and think of a difficult time. Difficulties can be seen as a gift; an error can be seen as a learning experience, and failure as success. Through our choice, we determine whether we live our life with gratitude and dignity or with bitterness.   With gratitude we have one of the most important spiritual tools for understanding and accepting life.

The greatest thing is to give thanks for everything. He who has learned this knows what it means to live. He has penetrated the whole mystery of life:

giving thanks for everything.

~ **Albert Schweitzer, recipient of the 1952 Nobel Peace Prize for his book *Reverence for Life*.**

You say grace before meals. All right. But I say grace before the concert and the opera, and grace before the play and pantomime, and grace before I open a book, and grace before sketching, painting, and swimming, fencing, boxing, walking, playing, dancing, and grace before I dip the pen in ink.

~ **G. K. Chesterton, English writer, 1874-1936**

"...give thanks in all circumstances..."

~ **1 Thessalonians 5:18**

Listen – Ting

Traditional script	Simplified script
Left side top: ear	Left: mouth
Left side bottom: scholar	Right: discerning
Right side: refinement	

There are two ways to write the character for "listen." In the 1950s the Chinese government decided to simplify some of the most difficult Chinese characters to make it easier to achieve literacy for the Chinese people. You can understand why they simplified the script when you see the two characters for "listen" side by side. It was simplified from twenty-two strokes down to six.

The left side of the traditional script version is a bit comic – there is a scholar on the bottom with a huge ear on the top. The right side has the character for refinement, which also means "straight" or "moral" on the top, and the heart character on the bottom. To summarize the character, it represents a scholar or disciple who is listening carefully (with that big ear) in order to refine the virtue that comes from the heart.

The character was shortened in the 1950s by putting the character for "mouth" on the left, and the character for "discerning" on the right, or you could say "to discern what comes from the mouth" means you are actively listening. It makes sense, of course, but I was much amused to note that in the past the character showed people listening with their ears, and in the character used now it might be misconstrued that we listen with our mouths!

When Spring comes to Shanghai, I get the feeling that an artist has gently spread a light wash of spring green over the whole city. The willows, which shyly let us see their tightly rolled spring green leaves as spring approaches all of a sudden let go and there is a celebration of vibrating green everywhere, especially in the parks. This green wave often happens around Saint Patrick's Day, and it would seem that the trees want to encourage us with their energy of new life and growth.

I love to stand outside in the spring when it is warm, and feel the golden sun and the incredible emerald dance of the willows and grass. I find that I can almost hear the growing going on, and the festivity of green in the park. This kind of listening is a spiritual listening which nourishes your heart.

Listening is much more than allowing another to talk while waiting for a chance to respond. Listening is paying full attention to others and welcoming them into our very beings. The beauty of listening is that those who are listened to start feeling accepted, start taking their words more seriously and discovering their true selves. Listening is a form of spiritual hospitality by which you invite strangers to become friends, to get to know their inner selves more fully, and even dare to be silent with you.
~ **Henri Nouwen, Dutch theologian and author, 1932-1996**

Music makes an altar out of our ears. A single struck tone, a note blown from a flute, can flush the body with goodness.
~ **W. A. Mathieu, musician and author**

In Old World Christian countries, noon was the classic time to pray the Angelus, a prayer of adoration in celebration of the Incarnation of Christ. The Angelus bells would ring at noon across town and cities. People would stop whatever they were doing, stand, turn to the sound of the bells and observe a minute of silent prayer.
~ Joseph Nassal and Nancy Burke, authors of *How To Pray*

Come, all you who are thirsty,
    come to the waters;
    and you who have no money,
    come, buy and eat!
    Come, buy wine and milk
    without money and without cost.
Why spend money on what is not bread,
    and your labor on what does not satisfy?
    Listen, listen to me, and eat what is good,
    and your soul will delight in the richest of fare.
Give ear and come to me;
    hear me, that your soul may live.
    I will make an everlasting covenant with you,
    my faithful love promised to David.

~ Isaiah 55:1-3

Simple - Jian

Top: bamboo, grass

Outer frame: door

Inner "window": the sun

With bamboo leaves overhead, we see the sun coming into the room through a space in the door.

Simplicity is a wonderful thing. Everyone who has to move their house to another city or apartment knows all about this. All that clutter and "stuff." What is worth moving? The Chinese say that when Confucius moved, he only moved books, and that his books filled a big ox cart.

This character is now used to describe the bamboo strips that were sewn together to make books in ancient times. The leaves depicted on the top show the bamboo origins. The bottom part is a phonetic piece which also really deepens the meaning, because it depicts the sun shining in through a door. It represents "the space in between." The space in between things is important – when there isn't much of it, you feel crowded.

When we begin to learn a skill, we tend to overdo it. I remember making cookies with a friend. In her zeal to make them "special" she added chocolate chips, raisins, spices, cherries and nuts of various sorts. On its own each ingredient was tasty, but crowded into the same cookie the result was almost inedible.   No space in between.

The simple spaces between characters and the pauses in music are critical. Some of the deepest poetry, like the poems of the Tang Dynasty, have just a few lines with few words, and lots of "space in between."

Jesus understood this – he instructed his disciples that when they pray they are "not to heap up empty phrases." They were also encouraged to live simply: "Freely you have received, freely give. Do not take along any gold or silver or copper in your belts; take no bag for the journey, or extra tunic, or sandals or a staff; for the worker is worth his keep."
(Matthew 10:8-10)

As you simplify your life, the laws of the universe will be simpler; solitude will not be solitude, poverty will not be poverty, nor weakness weakness.
~ **Henry David Thoreau,**

Everything should be made as simple as possible, but not simpler
~ **Albert Einstein, 1879 – 1955**

And my favorite quote that makes me laugh, to use to help simplify your wardrobe and decide which clothes to get rid of from your clothes closet:

"Never wear anything that panics the cat."
~ **P.J. O'Rourke, American political satirist, journalist, and author.**

Fear – Ju

Left side: vertical style heart

Right side: a falcon, with two eyes on the top

The Chinese character for "fear" is pronounced "joo", and is usually followed by the character *pa* which also means "fear."

How interesting to find a bird of prey watching carefully for danger in this character. When I am afraid, looking back and forth scanning for danger is what I do with my eyes, but the painful part is not in my eyes but in my heart. The eyes just scan. The heart is the place where you feel concern.

Shanghai is a southern city, and we often have stormy weather in March. Maybe even some thunder. I thought of thunder, and remembered how our dog Bear used to leap in a perfect arc and dive under the covers when there was thunder, and how she used to hide under the bed and cry during the thunderous Chinese New Year fireworks. She also cried when I played the suona (a Chinese musical instrument a lot like the chanter part of the Scottish bagpipe) which made it difficult to tell if I was playing on key or not! Bear was mostly brave, but loud noises left her cowering under the bed.

When I was a child I was afraid of many things. Because I lived in New York City, I was mostly afraid that a robber would break into our apartment and then kill me, so I even had an escape plan to hide in a closet where no one would find me. I would practice to make sure I could get up to the top of the closet and hide in as few seconds as possible, a procedure much like the nuclear bomb drills we had in school in the 1960s when we were required to hide under our desks upon a moments notice.   My neighborhood wasn't the safest. But ultimately I found that my early unsafe environment gave me some strength to cope with "scary places."

Jesus often went to scary places. He was constantly acting in ways outside of what was considered respectable. He would touch corpses, talk to lepers, chat with outcasts like tax collectors, who collaborated with the hated Romans, or with prostitutes, and in the end he faced death alone. Buddhist monks in the Tibetan tradition make a point to practice meditation in scary places, and sometimes sit in a cemetery to contemplate death.

It may seem strange that going to the places that scare you can develop your spiritual strength, but this is one practice that is worth thinking about. When we address our fear, open ourselves to pain, and let ourselves be vulnerable with someone who scares us or is suffering, we are living in the heart of compassion, which will ultimately transform us.

Mother Teresa is one who went to the scary places and through her interest, concern and love the face of Christ and the compassionate hands of God were manifested for many who were suffering greatly. For us, considering what scares us and what makes us anxious is a good way to find a new path for spiritual development.

Even though I walk
through the valley of the shadow of death,
I will fear no evil,
for you are with me;
your rod and your staff,
they comfort me.
~ Psalm 23:4

"The only thing we have to fear is fear itself - nameless, unreasoning, unjustified, terror which paralyzes needed efforts to convert retreat into advance."

~ President Franklin D. Roosevelt - First Inaugural Address, 1933

Silence – Jing

Left top: lush growth

Left bottom: burning red

**Right: two hands struggling, often representing
the concept of competition**

The character on the left can stand by itself and has two meanings – one is "purity" and the other is to "think vividly." The right side carries the meaning of competition. Whoever thought of this character must have had experience with meditation, because in meditation there can be a real struggle between our thoughts and the no-thought state of pure silent peace.

I have a few friends who like to keep their television on all the time. They have various reasons. One loves the news. Another lives alone in the country and feels lonely, so the sound of someone talking soothes and calms her. Yet another uses the sound of the television to block the racket of the traffic in the street outside his window.

We have many more sounds in our lives than our ancestors did. Music or news in the car or kitchen, elevators, or department stores fills our minds with sound and advertisements. In China the loudspeakers are turned up full blast outside shops, repeating the same patter over and over for the "happy and noisy" group feeling people here crave. (It is called *re-nao*, or "heat and noise.")   Even our tape players are called "boom boxes," as if we need any more noise and "boom." We stick earphones in our ears, turn up the volume on our iPods and go out jogging. Noise, music, TV, radio and public address systems keep us from having to listen to ourselves and to nature. When the house is empty I find myself thinking about the silence and feeling a little lonely. Do I turn on the TV, or do I welcome in the silence?

Greek Orthodox theologians in the 14th century had a principle of theology. They felt that any statement about God should have two aspects. The first was that the statement should be paradoxical so we are always reminded that God cannot fit into our limited human perception. The second was that the statement should lead us into the speechless awe of silence.

Ralph Waldo Emerson once said that he liked the silent church before the service began better than the preaching. A modern day Benedictine monk, David Steindl-Rast, calls the space that we create in silence "God bathing," the still, silent and peaceful place where we "bathe" in the presence of God. Silence is restoring. And if you have silence in your mind without struggling, then you are in your truest nature sitting in the presence of God.

It is not speaking that breaks our silence, but the anxiety to be heard.
~ Thomas Merton, 1915-1968, Trappist monk and author

Be still, and know that I am God
~ Psalm 46:10

God is the friend of silence. See how nature - trees, flowers, grass - grow in silence; see the stars, the moon, the sun, how they move in silence. Is not our mission to give God to the poor in the slums? Not a dead God, but a living, loving God. The more we receive in silent prayer, the more we can give in our active life. We need silence to be able to touch souls. The essential thing is not what we say, but what God says to us and through us. All our words will be useless unless they come from within - words which do not give the light of Christ increase the darkness. **~ Mother Theresa**

Silence is a source of great strength.
~ Laozi (Lao Tzu), 600 BC-531 BCE

Why are you so afraid of silence,
silence is the root of everything.
If you spiral into its void,
a hundred voices will thunder messages you long to hear.

~ **Rumi, Persian mystic, 1207-1273**

Principle - Li

Left: King
Right: Inner or Inside

A character with many meanings – they include 1) to work jade, 2) texture or grain, 3) principle, reason, logic, 4) manage, administer 5) arrange, 6) acknowledge, respond

What a beauty this character is, with the root character for "king" (pronounced wah-ng) on the left, and a *li* phonetic character on the right adding a bit of its own meaning of "inner" or "inside".   The kingly or sovereign principles to be found inside us, this is our *li*.

Sitting in a garden, smelling the scent of flowers blooming in beautiful colors or listening to the birds sing and call each other as they flit in and out of the trees can all bring the transcendent to mind. Hearing the sound of the rushing brook, seeing the fresh greenness of a hillside in spring, or even watching the snow fall on the mountain peaks, the divine presence can be perceived in the world.

And the divine presence is manifested too in a smile, a generous gesture, a hug, kind words, the gift of a flower, maybe a Valentine, and even a baby who offers you their chewed cookie! As it is expressed in Ephesians, God is "over all and through all and in all."   When we aren't too overwhelmed with our work or life, what a joyous feeling we can have to radiate the *Li*, the witness of the divine presence, to those around us.

So it is there; all we have to do is spot it and notice it as we go through our day, and we will be able to revel in all the ways the divine presence is felt both inside and outside.

One year I visited a small temple in the outskirts of Luoyang and discovered that one of the dusty side halls was filled with vendors selling the usual temple souvenirs. That was an ordinary temple sight, but off to one side, lined up on a railing, was one small sculpture after another of historical and mythical heroes and saints, all made of the roots and branches of cypress trees. A few of the older trees lining the pathways of the temple had died and been cut down. No doubt the trunks of the trees had been incorporated into the reconstruction that was going on at the temple. But the roots and branches, unsuitable for construction, had been salvaged and transformed into a host of familiar worthies and statues.

I was transfixed. The sculptor was there, a short jolly man, finishing and polishing the pieces while he happily chatted with the visitors. He told us that he could see the form in each piece through following the grain of the wood, and it just carved itself. I love the idea of God's presence lying within us like the rings and lines in the grain of wood.

I was reading recently how the ancient carvers of jade in China, like the best sculptors from all ages, worked with the natural lines of the stone to carve the refined pieces that were used in ceremonies or for artistic purposes. They too had sought out the natural lines that made a creation of exceptional natural grace. The word they used for the natural lines of the jade was *li*, the character you see above. The word *li* evolved over time to have many meanings.

It might be a good idea for society to dig back into this study – the study of how to encourage the *li*, the natural decency and goodness of people, to uncover and encourage a more empathetic spirituality like that given in the Golden Rule. Jesus pointed to rising above and beyond selfishness to an all-encompassing compassion and love as his "Way," the heart of his teaching.

The Golden Rule is one of the religious principles that, like the "li" lines in jade, extend to every part of the globe, beyond change and time.

The Golden Rule

Christianity

In everything, do to others as you would have them do to you; for this is the law and the prophets.
~ Jesus, Matthew 7:12

Baha'i Faith

Lay not on any soul a load that you would not wish to be laid upon you, and desire not for anyone the things you would not desire for yourself.
~ Baha'u'llah, Gleanings

Buddhism

Treat not others in ways that you yourself would find hurtful.
~ The Buddha, Udana-Varga 5.18

Confucianism

One word which sums up the basis of all good conduct....loving-kindness. Do not do to others what you do not want done to yourself.
~ Confucius, Analects 15.23

Daoism (Taoism)

Regard your neighbour's gain as your own gain and your neighbor's loss as your own loss.
~ Lao Tzu, Tai Shang Kan Ying Pian, 213-218

Hinduism

This is the sum of duty: do not do to others what would cause pain if done to you.
~ Mahabharata 5:1517

Islam

Not one of you truly believes until you wish for others what you wish for yourself.

~ The Prophet Muhammad, Hadith

Judaism

What is hateful to you, do not do to your neighbour. This is the whole Torah; all the rest is commentary. Go and learn it.

~ Hillel, Talmud, Shabbath 31a

Native American Spirituality

We are as much alive as we keep the earth alive.

~ Chief Dan George

Sikhism

I am a stranger to no one; and no one is a stranger to me.

Indeed, I am a friend to all.

~ Guru Granth Sahib

Gift - Li

Left: omen/revelations

Right: a *dou*, kind of vessel used in worship

The first character of the word for gift (*li wu*) is *li* and it has a very complicated set of meanings. Confucius, the great philosopher whose thought spread and transformed Asia five hundred years before Jesus' birth, often discussed this *li*. I don't want to try to tackle Confucius here, but want to look at the pieces of the character in their simplest form - the part on the left means revelations, and the right side pictures a sacrificial vessel used for worship. Revelations from the vessel used for worship, this is a gift!

I remember well a beautiful spring morning in Chong Qing. Peter and I walked outside as the darkness gave way to spring light. It was nice to have his big, warm hand around my hand keeping it warm. The air had a nip, but without any doubt at all, spring was all around us, and it would become a sunny day. The birds sang dozens of different songs, chirps, and tweets, and the plum blossoms, tissue thin, shone in the early morning light. The ground under the cherry trees was covered in red petals that had dropped in the rain, and it looked like the ground here after New Year's Eve, covered in the remains of the red paper coating of fireworks. But this wasn't the result of human celebration, it was spring fireworks at its best, nature's own celebration. And what is better than a walk in the spring air with someone you love?

Henri Nouwen wrote about life as a gift in his beautiful book, "Life of the Beloved." This is one of those deep thoughts, abstract, and therefore a little harder to grasp. I so often think of what someone has to give to this world as being their skills or talents, but there is a deep truth in what Nouwen says that the real gift is who we are. Our gift to each other is that we can share revelations from our earthly vessel.

First of all, our life itself is the greatest gift to give – something we constantly forget. When we think about our being given to each other, what comes immediately to mind are our unique talents: those abilities to do special things especially well. You and I have spoken about this quite often. "What is our unique talent?" we asked. However, when focusing on talents, we tend to forget that our real gift is not so much what we can do, but who we are. The real question is not "What can we offer each other?" but "Who can we be for each other?" No doubt, it is wonderful when we can repair something for a neighbor, give helpful advice to a friend, offer wise counsel to a colleague, bring healing to a patient, or announce good news to a parishioner, but there is a greater gift than all of this. It is the gift of our own life that shines through all we do. As I grow older, I discover more and more that the greatest gift I have to offer is my own joy of living, my own inner peace, my own silence and solitude, my own sense of well-being. When I ask myself, "Who helps me the most?" I must answer, "The one who is willing to share his or her life with me."

It is worthwhile making a distinction between talents and gifts. More important than our talents are our gifts. We may have only a few talents, but we have many gifts. Our gifts are the many ways in which we express our humanity. They are part of who we are: friendship, kindness, patience, joy, peace, forgiveness, gentleness, love, hope, trust, and many others. These are the true gifts we have to offer to each other. ~ **Henri Nouwen, Dutch priest and author of "Life of the Beloved" (1932-1996)**

Tolerance – Rong

Top: the dot and line are a cover
Middle: two drops of water, an alternate writing
of the character for water
Bottom: a mouth, together with the middle section meaning "a valley."

The character for "tolerance" depicts water coming through the mouth of a ravine on the bottom with a cover on top. Even though the cover is there, the water comes pouring through in spite of it all, the living water of tolerance and openness.

I have been thinking about my neighborhood when I was a child lately. I took a bus to school, since it was more than a mile away, and sometimes I would walk home if the weather was good and I felt like walking. I usually stuck to Broadway, which was bustling with small shops with windows to look in and interesting people to watch. Sometimes I walked home on Riverside Drive, which was quite deserted because one side was a park, and the other side had a few doorways to apartment buildings, but not much else. Walking there always made me a little anxious for fear that I would run into someone who was unfriendly.

Mystery arrived at a walled garden in front of an old stone building partway home, and my brother and I liked to peek in. Inside was an enormous statue of an Asian person with a big grass hat towering above us, and my brother liked to try to scare me by saying that the statue was real and was going to come after me. Thank goodness I knew it was a statue! Besides, the statue didn't look threatening, just tall. I didn't know the significance of the statue; I just knew the real person must have been kind to children, because I wasn't afraid.

I left New York City when I graduated from high school, and didn't have much time there after that. I occasionally get back to the neighborhood when I am visiting a dear friend who lives down the street, but I was moved to find a description of the statue, which is no longer behind a wall but out in the street easily visible by all who pass by, written by Madeleine L'Engle, who lived in the same neighborhood.

When I walk my dog at night, the route on the way home takes me past a Buddhist temple with a terrace on which stands a huge statue of Saint Shinran Shonin, a Buddhist saint of the twelfth century. This particular statue was in Hiroshima when the bomb fell, and was sent by the Buddhists of that city to the Buddhists in New York as a symbol of forgiveness and hope. Each night as my dog and I walk by the great statue, the huge bulk of metal wearing a patina I have never seen on another statue, I say, "Good night Saint Shinran. Forgive us and help us," and for me, at that moment, Saint Shinran is one of God's angels. Am I worshipping a pagan saint? A lifeless hunk of metal? No! It is an attitude of heart, a part of turning to Christ.

I rejoice to read in William Johnstone's The Inner Eye of Love that Saint Shinran rebelled against legalism and proclaimed "the preeminence of faith and grace," and that "he has been frequently compared to Martin Luther."
~ **Madeleine L'Engle, American author of many books for adults, children, and young adults, including "A Wrinkle in Time," 1918-2007**

What is tolerance? It is the consequence of humanity. We are all formed of frailty and error; let us pardon reciprocally each other's folly - that is the first law of nature.
~ **Voltaire, French Enlightenment writer and philosopher, 1694-1778**

The mark of a moderate man is freedom from his own ideas. Tolerant like the sky, all-pervading like sunlight, firm like a mountain, supple like a tree in the wind, he has no destination in view and makes use of anything life happens to bring his way. Nothing is impossible for him. Because he has let go, he can care for the people's welfare as a mother cares for her child.

~ Laozi, Tao De Ching (Dao De Jing)

I have a wonderful friend named Andu who lives deep in the back alleys behind the Lama Temple in Beijing who does calligraphy and oil paintings in a style distinctly his own, but which might be called "modern traditional!" He often paints lotus flowers to commemorate his mother, whose name meant Lotus, and who passed away during the Cultural Revolution. I have a beautiful calligraphy scroll that he painted and so kindly gave to me, which says "*you rong nai da*," to be tolerant (magnanimous, forgiving), this is greatness."

有容乃大- You Rong Nai Da

"To be tolerant, this is greatness"

Andu, modern calligrapher, Beijing

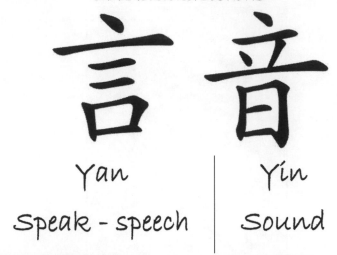

Yan

Speak - speech

Yin

Sound

Have you ever thought of words as vapors that come from your mouth? In this character, the box at the bottom is a mouth, with vapors going up and out.

I love the mouth in this form, with the sound rising out so you can see it. It is reminiscent of being able to see your breath outside when the air is cold. A similar character expands the meaning to include all sound.

Yin means "sound".

The mouth – which looks like a window at the bottom of this character – has something in it!   And the sounds coming out are more elaborate! The line through the mouth-box is described as a tongue, words, and is also thought to be the numeral one, which represents heaven or the divine. All by itself the window means the "sun".   So there it is, the meaning deepens and the light that can be heard becomes sound.

This character is used in combinations of characters referring to music. Isn't it a wonderful thought to see music as the light that becomes sound? No matter where you are, in a church, temple, or even just outside, if you can hear the sound of sacred music, your spirit feels lifted, and you are put in touch again with your divine foundation. Here the peace, calm, solace, and a deeper sense of well-being that comes from being connected with the sacred can be felt.

Sound and the divine have a natural connection that we can experience if we listen carefully. We are being whispered to all the time by the universe in the singing of the birds at the turn of day, the sound of the sea, the wind in the mountains or blowing through a field of corn, and the sound of people in the market. Isn't it wonderful to have ears and the ability to hear?

Courage – Yong

Top and Center: "to bud" or "burst forth"

Bottom: a plow, which represents "strength"

It almost looks like it is bursting forth from the middle part, which in ancient times meant "divine" or "center", but also later came to mean "bell."

Bursting forth from your divine center with strength – this is courage. The famous Chinese philosopher Mencius pointed out that true courage does not just require fearless action, but also the wisdom that comes from one's divine center to know what is and what is not to be feared.

When I think of courage I usually think of someone else! Courage is a word that I associate with brave warriors in battle. They are courageous because they move forward in spite of their fear, or even oblivious to their fear. Courage goes against a basic intuition, which is to want to protect ourselves. When we are afraid we draw back. Having courage means pressing forward in the face of fear. It doesn't have to be in a military battle. It happens in everyday life.

I recently was in Nanjing, visiting the Amity Foundation, one of China's first NGOs that began in the 1980s, carrying out projects all over China to promote education, social services, health, and rural development. Visiting the

"House of Blessings," where graduates of special education schools around Nanjing find simple work to do, we found young adults baking bread and cookies. They are doing such a good job that people who have tried their baked goods are asking for more. These young people, who are used to staying at home and not participating in society are courageous to leave their homes and participate in a job.

Someone waiting for a diagnosis of their illness can reveal courage. Someone moving from a house they have lived in for 20 years can show courage when they take that step. Someone who has had a death in the family or has had a beloved friend die shows courage when they face the future without their loved one. A young person who refuses to smoke with their friends is showing real courage, because he or she stands up to pressure to conform.

Courage is contagious. Researching Helen Keller, whose life is a tale of courage from beginning to end, I found a simple story from the New York Times in 1913. The report was about a man who had his leg amputated after a coal mining accident who was wishing he would die. When he heard the story of Helen Keller and her courage, he was reported to have said, "Well, if that deaf, dumb, and blind girl can do so much for herself and others, you bet I'll find a way to get along." The newspaper reports that Helen Keller heard of the incident, and sent the miner $20 with a note saying, "For the man in the hospital who must begin life over again heavily handicapped – From your friend, Helen Keller."

Courage is not simply one of the virtues, but the form of every virtue at the testing point.
~ **C. S. Lewis, British theologian and author 1898-1963**

Courage is almost a contradiction in terms. It means a strong desire to live taking the form of readiness to die. ~ **G. K. Chesterton, English writer, 1874-1936**

Kind – Shan

Top: sheep

Bottom: words

The top part of this character represents a sheep, known for its gentleness. The bottom is an altered form of the character for "words." Gentle words are kind words.

Old Lu was a company driver who often drove my children to town in his van. He was very kind, patient and understanding. One day when we were driving down a small one-way lane, a big truck came around the corner going in the wrong direction. We were late, and gnashing our teeth. Peter and I were doing the usual Western practice of muttering condemnation at the truck driver. Old Lu, smiling sweetly, backed up down the street so the truck could drive through. We said, "Why are you backing up? It's not your fault. The other driver is wrong. *He* should back up." Old Lu smiled his wisdom smile and said, "Look, the truck is from out of town. Maybe he has lost his way. He has probably been driving all day."

I have often reflected that "kind" is a word that doesn't have much depth to it. Perhaps it is because we have the phrase "How kind of you" in English, which is just a form and doesn't necessarily carry much weight. Or maybe because the word "kind" has other meanings, like "variety" or "manner." It just doesn't have much punch as a word. But kindness is one of the primary attributes of Jesus and other people of great depth who are filled with divine wisdom.

Kindness is born from the willingness to look deeply at someone or some situation and make the effort to understand the other person's point of view. It is also the sign of a compassionate heart, of someone who sees the suffering of others and has a merciful attitude. When you meet someone who is kind, you have met a divine emissary on this earth.

Be kind and merciful.
Let no one ever come to you
    without leaving better and happier.
Be a living expression of God's kindness.
Kindness in your face,
Kindness in your eyes,
Kindness in your smile,
Kindness in your warm greeting.
Kindness has converted more people than zeal, science, or eloquence.
~ **Mother Teresa**

Kindness is the language which the deaf can hear and the blind can see.
~ **Mark Twain, (1835-1910)**

The ideas that have lighted my way have been kindness, beauty and truth."
~ **Albert Einstein**

Without the Tao,
Kindness and compassion are replaced by law and justice;
Faith and trust are supplanted by ritual and ceremony.
~ **Laozi (Lao Tzu)**

Constant kindness can accomplish much. As the sun makes ice melt, kindness causes misunderstanding, mistrust, and hostility to evaporate.
~ **Albert Schweitzer, theologian, musician, philosopher, and physician (1875-1965)**

My religion is very simple. My religion is kindness.
~ **Dalai Lama**

The Way or Essence – Dao (Tao)

Right: warrior

Left: "moving forward"

The right side of this character is a warrior – you can almost imagine his face with his fancy hat sporting feathery plumes on top. Combined with the left-hand character for "moving forward", resembling a foot in motion, we see the leader whose feet forge ahead. But this character is not just referring to following or leading. In ancient times, the leaders were not just military or martial leaders but also priests, who led in spiritual ways. So the character evolved into "The Way", and is used in Chinese to describe the essence of all religion – The Dao.

For Christians in China, to "preach a sermon" is translated as "to speak the Dao". Buddhists and followers of Daoism also use the character to describe the "way", the essence or truth of their religion. The early translators of the Bible in China, who understood the deeper meaning of the character Dao, picked it as representing most closely "the Word", and so the first line of John's gospel in Chinese reads: "In the beginning was the Dao."

Essence is the most significant quality or nature of something.

When Jesus was asked by religious scholars of the time for the essence of his faith and the most important commandment, he answered "to love God and love your neighbor as yourself." Jesus spent many hours teaching stories and parables to help his disciples develop an awareness of these two essential things – God's love for humanity and the need for people to accept that love and let it flow through them like water through a channel.

Tea in a cup is a wonderful symbol for religion and culture. If you think of the tea as the essential and basic teachings of Jesus, then the cup can be thought of as culture. Without the cup, the tea would spill and be lost. The cup that contains the tea allows us to taste it. A cup may come in many different shapes, sizes and patterns, but it does not change what the tea is: the essence of the tea remains the same, regardless of the cup that contains it. Religious and spiritual teachings are always held in a cup – they are expressed in and through a culture. But what is essential about those teachings is the same in all cultures.

I remember reading about a group of theologians from the west who visited an Orthodox Church monastery in Israel. At some point in their visit, the Western theologians said they would like to pray with their colleagues for peace. The monks looked quizzical, and asked repeatedly if that was what they were thinking. It was. So then the monks began to change their clothes and put on special liturgical gowns, setting up the altar, and lighting candles. The request for what was meant as "something simple" was put in a much more serious light with a change of clothes, setting up of altar, and preparations for a serious time of prayer. Was one right and the other wrong? None of the theologians thought so, although the Westerners were a bit taken aback. Prayer for peace is just that no matter what the form, traditional or informal.

The essence of the tea, the teachings of Jesus, is beyond culture. It is so easy to focus on "how to do it" than to focus on "what to do". Ceremonies, rituals, traditions, and "flavors" of religion and denominations are other examples of this. Overly emphasizing whether we kneel, whether the priest kisses the altar or not during the mass, have a weekly altar call, whether there are candles or incense, nothing hanging on the walls or many stained glass windows, is to focus on the cup, and it can be easy to forget the tea. It is possible to have an empty cup or to forget to sip the tea, to let the tea go cold, or only hold the cup. The forms are not the essence of religion, and it is possible that they can become distractions to the real essence, the Dao, the real message of the teaching – to love God and love our neighbors as ourselves, This teaching needs a cup – whether simply or beautifully painted - if its liquid spirit is to be shared.

Blessings, Abundance – Fu

Left side: symbolizing things of the spirit, revelations, or God

Right side top: a mouth with a horizontal line, the character for "one", above it.

Right bottom: A field

The Chinese character *fu* (pronounced "foo") is an ancient one. In the oldest script, the character looks like two hands putting wine on an altar, to show a petitioner offering wine to God, asking God for a blessing. *Fu* is also used in words for good fortune or happiness.

In modern China, most people think of this character in a material way, and often you can see someone with a necklace or a piece of calligraphy with this character written as a prayer for material blessing and prosperity.

When society was mostly agricultural, "wealth" meant many crops, full barns, and freedom from hunger. So you can see the meaning here, a field full of crops, a mouth, and "one" or "united" with heaven, the source of abundance. About 3,500 years ago, the Chinese classical book *The Book of History* listed five types of blessings: long life, wealth, peace, virtue, and dying a natural death.   It is interesting to think about what would be on a list in the 21st century.

"Blessings" are not always what we expect them to be. There is a famous

Chinese story about a father and son in a town whose horse ran away, but came back to the village accompanied by some wild horses. The father and son managed to catch one of them. Everyone told the father, "You have been blessed to catch such a fine horse!"

He said, "Well, we'll see." His son began to train the horse to use him in the fields but had an accident and broke his leg.

The villagers said, "Oh, such bad luck that your son broke his leg!"

The father said, "Well, we'll see." The Emperor sent messengers to the village to draft all able-bodied young men for the army. The man's son couldn't go, since he had a broken leg.

The villagers said, "Oh my, you have had such good fortune to be able to keep your son at home!"

The father just smiled and said again, "We'll see."

Often we don't realize a blessing until we can look back. After a hurricane when the power is out in your house, you can appreciate the blessing of electricity and all it does for you. You might be transferred to a remote desert for a new job and miss the hustle and bustle of the city, but you might also find that the desert has its own amazing splendor and come to see the move as a blessing. It may seem strange on first thought, but sometimes what seems to be a difficult or "bad" situation may turn into something you see as a "blessing" later on.

Blessed are the poor in spirit, for theirs is the
    kingdom of heaven.
Blessed are those who mourn, for they will be comforted.
Blessed are the meek, for they will inherit the earth.
Blessed are those who hunger and thirst for
    righteousness, for they will be filled.
Blessed are the merciful, for they will be shown mercy.
Blessed are the pure in heart, for they will see God.

Blessed are the peacemakers,
for they will be called sons of God.
Blessed are those who are persecuted because of
righteousness, for theirs is the kingdom of heaven.
~ **Matthew 5: 3-10**

Just as the soft rains fill the streams,
pour into the rivers and join together in the oceans,
so may the power of every moment of your goodness
flow forth to awaken and heal all beings,
Those here now, those gone before, those yet to come.
...For all in whose heart dwells respect,
who follow the wisdom and compassion, of the Way,
May your life prosper in the four blessings
of old age, beauty, happiness and strength.
~ **Buddhist blessing**

Ren - Benevolence

Left: person
Right: the number two

The character for humaneness - benevolence is made up of two parts – a person on the left and the number *two* on the right. It takes two people in a relationship to discover benevolence. One is not enough.

When I had finished this book I sent it to a Chinese scholar whom I admire very much. He said, "The most important ideogram of all, "仁", is missing." As I thought about it, I knew he was right. So in this book, where I planned to have forty characters, there are actually forty-one.

If you want to light a Confucian scholar on fire, ask them about the character *ren* (also written as *jen*, since the sound is in between the *r* and *j* sounds of English). *Ren* is the central concept of Confucian thinking, and some say everything he wrote centered around *ren*, which I like to define as deep concern for the welfare of others. In ancient times, it described the kindness and care an ideal ruler had for his subjects. Confucius talked about it in the concept of the extended family, and the philosopher Mozi argued that this concern for the welfare of others should even extend to the world, and to the universe.

I like simple explanations! When I had the chance, I asked Granny Han, the grandmother who founded a school for special ed children in a poor coal mining town, who is the soul of kindness, benevolence, and compassion, (see page 5 in chapter one), to explain it to me and the class. She stood up at the blackboard and drew the character. "You see?" she said. "In this character on the right is the number "two." This line is you. The line below is me." She moved her chalk up and down between the two lines very slowly, punctuating her words. "I help you. You help me. I help you, and you help me." It is that spirit, the spirit of humaneness and benevolence that gives us depth to our humanity.

In the West we tend to focus on tasks and our work, focusing on achieving goals and "getting the work done." This can even sometimes become more important than rest, health, marriages and relationships with children. In the East, the focus is on nurturing relationships instead, and the group takes precedence over the individual. The task is secondary. It is not that the goal of a task is forgotten, but that it does not set the priorities. That difference in orientation is what makes it so hard to translate *ren*.

Ren, together with *Ci,* makes up the Chinese word for "compassion."

Fan Chi asked about humaneness (ren). The Master said it is loving people. Fan Chi asked about wisdom. The Master said it is knowing people." (Analects of Confucius XII.22)

Compassion – Ci

Top: lush

Bottom: heart

The ancient version of the character *Ci* * had the image of a "son" and a "daughter" cradled over the representation of a heart. The love a parent has for a child is deep, compassionate love. In the modern version of the character, the children, looking like two "E"s, are represented by the character for tender young grass, and carry the meaning of "lush." So this character reminds us that when we have that deep love and lush compassion of a parent for a child, not just for our own family, but for everyone in need, pain, or in sorrow, the Divine becomes visible in the world and we participate in the energy of God's love and compassion.

When I was in Sichuan after the big earthquake in 2008 helping to train counselors in post-traumatic stress psychology, I saw pictures of a local policewoman who had nursed many babies after the quake when things were still in chaos. The picture showed her with four babies in her arms, but she actually nursed many more infants than that. I thought of her because the

---

* Pronunciation: If you say the word "cats" you will discover the sound at the end of the word – "ts. If you add an "uh" sound after that, and you will have the proper pronunciation for "ci."

character has two children cradled near the heart. She cradled many more than that in her compassionate arms during those first days after the quake.

We also had news of Old Brother Wu, a member of the church in nearby Sui Ning, took his total life's savings of 10,000 rmb (about 1,400 USD) and generously gave all of it to the Red Cross to help the rescue teams who were digging people out of buildings. When the media asked him why he had given his entire savings away, he said "Jesus had compassion for all people, and that is what Christians do."

Some years ago I heard of two families in Nanjing who, when they discovered that their sons had been switched at birth in the hospital nursery, did not demand their sons be exchanged, but moved so they could be closer to each other and the boys could grow up in both families. Two babies with parents whose hearts were big enough to take in both children and another family too. I understand that the boys were the best of friends and free spirits, scooting back and forth between the two houses, deciding which dinner looked more delicious and spending the night at that house. The boys' parents showed real compassion for their children in their decision.

Compassion can arise in many situations, big and small, and there are many ways to show it. In Asia they have "seven offerings that cost nothing:" a compassionate eye, a smiling face, loving words, physical service, a warm heart, a seat, and a place for people to spend the night.

Universal – Ju Shi

Top: Hands giving	Character: symbol for 30 years -
Bottom: hands - lifting up meaning whole, entire	meaning a generation or an era

"Hands giving back and forth for generations" is the symbol that creates the idea of universality.

There are many ways to look at something, but the brain focuses more easily on details and differences than the larger picture. Perhaps that ability was honed during our hunter phase, when the hunter needed to identify the break in the monotonous prairie grasses to see where the deer was standing so he could find some meat for his family. Or possibly our ability to notice differences was strengthened when the broad field of grasses moved ever so slightly so people noticed the motion as a tiger crept in our direction. Or maybe we developed this capacity when we perceived fine distinctions in mushrooms to decide if the mushroom would poison us or not.

Because the brain focuses on detail, when we meet someone from a different culture or religion our mind instantly moves into noting the details and differences. Differences are fascinating. However, if they lead into intolerance, the result is sad.

People have a much harder time seeing similarities or universalities. Our educational system does not train us to look at the broader picture, and our brains do not naturally flow in this direction, although it is easier for some people than others.   In religion and spirituality the move to a broader view of what they share in common will bring us to a higher spiritual view that is lit with tolerance and acceptance.

Looking at similarities and the broader picture is more encouraging, kinder, a more graceful way to be with others, truly emanating from our spiritual core. What will be useful for us to "lift up, with hands giving from generation to generation" will be the larger picture of religion, where we can share, hand to hand, our ideas concerning generosity, love, compassion, virtue, patience, truth, kindness, understanding, forgiveness, and wisdom.

For us there is one God, the Father, from whom are all things and for whom we exist...
~ 1 Corinthians 8:6

He is the one God hidden in all beings, all-pervading, the Self within all beings, watching over all worlds, dwelling in all beings, the witness, the perceiver.
~ Hinduism, Svetasvatara Upanishad 6:11

There is but one God whose name is true. He is the creator, immortal, unborn, self-existent.
~ Sikhism, The Japji

Practice – Xiu Xing

Left side: person	**Left side:** step
Right side: originating from an ancient word for a person crossing a stream with a stick in their hand	**Right side:** stop
	Step and Stop in sequence indicate motion

When we practice, we "step and stop", and do it all over again. Sometimes we need help along the way, and a "stick" of some sort will keep us from falling on our way.

I suspect that the stick in the hand of the one crossing the river represents spiritual practice. The fact is that all the talk in the world about religion and spirituality get us nowhere unless we are moving, practicing, and integrating our developing spiritual understanding into our everyday lives.

I have been asked more than once by a Buddhist friend what my "spiritual practice" is. I like to change my practice so that I don't get bored. I have some rose beads made by Granny Han and her teachers and students that I like to use to pray the "I love you" prayer for everyone who comes to mind. I practice smiling at people, and have a prayer pot where I put things I want to pray about.

This is different from practicing the piano, which might (or for some might not) be mechanical and done out of a sense of obligation. When we practice a skill, we are usually thinking about succeeding or failing to attain a new level of ability.

Spiritual practice is not so much something in which you can fail – but more something that is outside of failure and success. It is training oneself in how to look at the world. It is tweaking, attending to, and polishing our character, and if we can do it out of the joy of it, and not out of guilt, it is one of the finest pleasures of life.

Wherein does religion consist? It consists in doing as little harm as possible, in doing good in abundance, in the practice of love, of compassion, of truthfulness and purity, in all the walks of life.
~ Taoism

To be a cause of healing to every sick one; a comforter for every sorrowful one; a pleasant water for every thirsty one; a heavenly table for every hungry one; a guide for every seeker... a light for every lamp; a herald to every yearning one for the kingdom of God.
~ Baha'I

First rectify thyself and then convert others. Take pity on orphans, assist widows; respect the old, be kind to children. Even the multifarious insects, herbs, and trees should not be injured. Be grieved at the misfortune of others and rejoice at their good luck. Assist those in need, and rescue those in danger. Regard your neighbor's gain as your own gain, and regard your neighbor's loss as your own loss. Do not call attention to the faults of others, nor boast of your own excellence. Stay (hold back) evil and promote goodness. Renounce much, accept little. Show endurance in humiliation and bear no grudge. Receive favors as if surprised. Extend your help without seeking reward. Give to others and do not regret or begrudge your liberality.
~ Taoism, T'ai-Shang Kan-Ying P'ien (176-262)

Here there is no Greek or Jew, circumcised or uncircumcised, barbarian, Scythian, slave or free, but Christ is all, and is in all.

Therefore, as God's chosen people, holy and dearly loved, clothe yourselves with compassion, kindness, humility, gentleness and patience. Bear with each other and forgive whatever grievances you may have against one another. Forgive as the Lord forgave you. And over all these virtues put on love, which binds them all together in perfect unity.

Let the peace of Christ rule in your hearts, since as members of one body you were called to peace. And be thankful. Let the word of Christ dwell in you richly as you teach and admonish one another with all wisdom, and as you sing psalms, hymns and spiritual songs with gratitude in your hearts to God. And whatever you do, whether in word or deed, do it all in the name of the Lord Jesus, giving thanks to God the Father through him.

~ **Colossians 3:11-17**

Mindfulness – Nian

Top - now, the present

Bottom - heart

The top part means Now.   The bottom part means Heart, which maybe could be better translated as Mind for us English speakers.   In this way, the character for "mindfulness" means Now Heart - Mind.

Mindfulness is about remembering to pay attention and remain aware. It also involves remembering to experience everything, and includes not trying to escape or deny feelings that are not so pleasant. Everything is a topic of mindfulness - pain and sorrow, the simple things we do that we usually don't notice, like taking hold of the door handle before opening the door, and also all the marvelous things in life.

Jesus told us, "Take no thought for the morrow." So we are asked not to worry about the future. Jesus told Peter, when asked how many times he had to forgive his brother, that he should forgive him seventy times seven. We are taught in this way to "Take no thought for the past," since we are being asked to let the past go. God's gift to us is not the past, nor the future, but this present moment, and Now is where we are called to find the Kingdom.

With mindfulness, we can enjoy the moment of Now that we have been given in each moment, whether we are stuck in traffic, washing dishes, eating a delicious meal, or even if it is just to open our mouth and enjoy a yawn.

"The kingdom of God is not coming with signs to be observed, nor will they say, 'Look, here it is!' or 'There!' for behold, the kingdom of God is in the midst of you."
~ **Luke 17: 20-21**

The Great Tao flows everywhere.
~ **Tao Te Ching**

We could say that the word mindfulness is pointing to being one with our experience, not dissociating, being right there when our hand touches the doorknob or the telephone rings or feelings of all kinds arise.
~ **Pema Chodron, Buddhist nun and author of** *When Things Fall Apart*

Charity, to Give Alms, to Bestow, to Abandon -

She

Left: a hand

Right: a phonetic

Helping others requires an open hand.

When we are born we are mostly aware of "me." In the womb we didn't have the chance to know much else. As a baby grows, there is a day when they offer something to their parents, and the parents' hearts leap because they know that their child is developing awareness of others, and is sharing their love.

The phonetic side of this character has ancient roots in characters for thatch and is a phonetic clue to help pronounce the character. In its modern form, the bottom part looks like a mouth with a tongue sticking out, and carries the meaning of "tongue."

I remember the day we went to a truck stop to have dinner, and one of our daughters, certainly not a year old yet, became intrigued by a man who looked a bit like a bearded leprechaun sitting nearby. My daughter, who had eyes like an elf herself, picked up a cracker and offered it to him. I was about to reach over and hold her hand back, since the cracker was soggy from being chewed on, but the leprechaun had accepted her soggy offering, and was happily munching away, smiling and laughing at the delightful gift that had just been bestowed on him by a fellow elf.

Babies can be wonderfully generous with no asking. As we get older, we are encouraged to be generous. Sometimes generousity comes naturally and sometimes we are forced unwillingly to give away something we don't want to give away, a cookie, or a bite of an ice cream cone. We are told that we will have some sort of reward if we give things away or show charity.

When someone is genuinely concerned with someone other than themselves, a deep level of spirituality has been attained. There is no question that people have a broadening of their spiritual understanding after having a child of their own, or finding a person whose needs you put ahead of your own, be it spouse, an older person who needs your help, or someone who is ill.

If we see someone who is suffering from loneliness, sadness, lack, hunger, or discrimination, then we have the opportunity to cheer them, give something that is needed, or champion those whose situation is unfair. When we recognize in others a situation or condition that we have also been through, then we can know and find ourselves too. We enter that place where we are joined in oneness, where we not only know ourselves but know the divine presence.

Humility – Qian Xu

Left: words

Right: uniting

(hands holding some grain)

Top: tiger

Bottom: hill

When we move towards unity, we are like the tiger on the hill, and have a higher vantage point to see the world, a rootedness, and a sense of self that springs from the divine within us.

After a year in China attending the Drum Tower District Number One Central Primary School, my daughters' Chinese had made great progress. They could communicate with their friends, and speak basic Mandarin. The first place they wanted to visit (after seeing family) when we went back to the US was their former elementary school, so we piled in the car and headed for their sweet red brick one story high Braeburn Elementary School and their delightful teachers from first grade.

One of the first things the teachers asked them to do was speak some Chinese for them. Out came some Chinese dialogues and jump rope rhymes they had learned from their friends, including one that began (in Chinese) "One day in Italy, the Italian King came to watch an opera…"

When they slowed to a halt, the teachers began to exclaim over them. "Oh, what good Chinese you have!" But shaking their hands left and right in the Chinese fashion, my daughters replied, "Oh no, not really, we have a long way to go."

This is what really stopped the show. The teachers looked horrified and proceeded to praise them up and down, and it dawned on me that what was the correct response in Chinese didn't work very well in English. What they were supposed to say was "thank you," but they had given the proper Chinese response instead, one that was considered very modest, humble and correct, but which didn't work in an English environment.

Humility and modesty seem to be "pale" virtues in the United States at this point in time. Being proud of your accomplishments and acknowledging what you are doing well is the current fashion. There is a lot to be said for it, especially in an educational setting and with children. But humility is the other end of the spectrum which brings about the balance needed to make progress. And it is one of the signs of spiritual greatness.

When a person is humble and deeply rooted in a spiritual path, they can find words that will unite all people instead of putting one person above another. Insisting that what we think is always right keeps us from having true strength. Like the tiger on the hill, a spiritual practice and path gives us a higher vantage point to see the world, a rootedness, and a sense of self that springs from the divine within us. With spiritual depth we can enjoy praise without being attached to it, and appreciate others for being the way they are and at whatever level they find themselves.

All who exalt themselves will be humbled, and all who humble themselves will be exalted.
~ **Matthew 23:12**

The sage puts himself last and finds himself in the foremost place.
~ **Tao Te Ching 7**

Would you become a pilgrim on the road of love? The first condition is that you make yourself humble as dust and ashes.
~ **Sufi tradition, Ansari of Herat (1006-1089)**

A man's pride shall bring him low: but honour shall uphold the humble in spirit.
~ **Book of Proverbs 29:23**

The highest degree of meekness consists in seeing, serving, honoring, and treating amiably, on occasion, those who are not to our taste, and who show themselves unfriendly, ungrateful, and troublesome to us.
~ **St. Francis De Sales, Catholic priest, 1567-1622   Patron saint of journalists and writers**

Humility like the darkness, reveals the heavenly lights.
~ **Henry David Thoreau, American Transcendentalist and author, 1817-1862**

We come nearest to the great when we are great in humility.
~ **Rabindranath Tagore (Bengali poet, winner of the 1913 Nobel Prize for Literature)**

Calm - Tai Ran

Top: a person with their hands out	**Combination character used in many words, no special meaning.**
Bottom: water slipping through	

Not much is more calming than water slipping through the fingers. Perhaps this is because it echoes the central spring of divine water that we all have flowing through us.

I searched through my dictionary to remind myself how to say the word "calm." There were several possibilities, but I discovered one I was not familiar with, so I called a friend who is an artist with words and excellent translator. "What is the meaning of *tai ran*?" I asked her.

She coughed and hummed and hah-ed. "I imagine this is not the word you are looking for. It would describe someone who would be exceedingly calm in the face of a huge storm, someone of great weight, like a mountain, but they might be thin. It is not about their weight in kilograms. It is about the weight of their spirit. Mount Tai is one of the Holy Mountains in China."

Searching in my mind for someone who might fit this description, I asked her, "Do you know anyone who is *tairan*?"

She laughed and said, "No. No one. This is the word that would be used to describe Jesus, or Moses, Buddha, or Laozi. It is not a word to be used lightly."

The character shows us water slipping through the hands: hands still, water in fluid motion. Movement and stillness, awake and asleep, resting and busy, we have these cycles throughout the day.

But there is another way of being, not of the physical aspect, but the spiritual, in which you can tap into a central spring of stillness and calm presence no matter what is happening.   In tune with something bigger than your self, this is where the Divine resonates and moves us to a spiritual response, to a kind reply, a smile, a caring gift, or a hug or squeeze on the arm.

In this place of calm we embody deep inner stillness no matter where we are, even if we are at a noisy meeting in a busy city. In this way we become like Mount Tai for everyone around us, a calm and spiritual presence that others can lean on and rest.

One day he got into a boat with his disciples, and he said to them, "Let us go across to the other side of the lake." So they set out, and as they sailed he fell asleep. And a windstorm came down on the lake, and they were filling with water and were in danger. And they went and woke him, saying, "Master, Master, we are perishing!" And he awoke and rebuked the wind and the raging waves, and they ceased, and there was a calm. He said to them, "Where is your faith?" And they were afraid, and they marveled, saying to one another, "Who then is this, that he commands even winds and water, and they obey him?"
~ Luke 8:22-25

Who is calm and quiet becomes the guide for the universe.
~ Tao Te Ching 45

Be still and know that I am God.
~ **Psalm 46:10**

I've built a grass hut where there's nothing of value...
The person in the hut lives here calmly,
not stuck to inside, outside, or inbetween...
Though the hut is small, it includes the entire world
In ten square feet, an old man illumines forms
and their nature.
~ **Zen poet Shi Tou, 700 – 790, translated by Taigen Daniel Leighton**

Never be in a hurry; do everything quietly and in a calm spirit. Do not lose your inner peace for anything whatsoever, even if your whole world seems upset.
~ **St. Francis de Sales, Catholic, 1567 – 1622, Patron saint of journalists and writers**

Observe – Guan

Left side: a stork

Right side: to see, a picture of an eye

The left part of the character is there for its phonetic sound, but it also means "stork", an animal known for its ability to stand perfectly still while observing what is happening underwater, and also known for its incredible grace and perfection of movement in flight. In ancient script, the right part of the character looks like a man with a big eye on top, like someone walking around staring at things. This half of the character means "to see" and is also used in other characters, including the characters for the ability to hear! I find that interesting, since being able to "see", to really hear someone and not just listen to sounds, is an important part of hearing. So, these two character parts put together make the word "guan" – used for words that describe the ability to see, observe, and meditate.

I was inspired that these characters embody principles I value highly – that seeing has two aspects, looking in and looking out, a flow that makes for a fuller development of individuals. We need to see – using our senses, looking out, and at the same time "to see", observe, and meditate, using our minds to analyze and contemplate what we have seen.

Many years ago I went to a conference at a center near the beach in Virginia. My daughters were very little then, and the whole family went along, including my mother, who helped us keep track of our daughters who loved to run around and play in the ocean. I don't remember the topic of the conference, but it included discussion of how to make changes in your life. There are two things I took back from this conference.

The first is that the beach off the coast of Virginia is mystically beautiful, and they have dolphins that swim right off the beach just beyond the surf. If you ever get near the Virginia coast you might want to make your way straight to the ocean's edge. But this is not the important point.

What I learned is if you want to change yourself for the better, both in your everyday life and in your spiritual life, you should practice the things that you are weak in. The thrust of what they taught us is this:

~If you tend to be **extroverted**, then you should try to develop your introverted aspect, by meditation, spending time alone, and quiet activities. If you are **introverted**, your challenge is to go out and spend more time with people, learn how to have more friends and participate in groups.

~If you are good at **detail**, then you should look to analysis of the big picture to develop yourself. If you are good at **analysis**, then spending time with the detail will round out your abilities.

--If you tend to be a person who perceives the world through the **five senses**, enjoying the tasting, touching, smelling, seeing, and hearing side of life, then you can cultivate yourself further by spending time thinking about and focusing on your perceptions. For those who perceive the world through the filter of their brain and are **thinkers**, growth will come through focusing on what you are feeling through your five senses.

~ And for those who usually prefer **schedules and agendas**, we can grow by taking time to relax and go with the flow, and likewise, for those of us who **go with the flow**, the benefit will come through setting a schedule or agenda and following it.

I have different friends I have known who have embodied this - I remember Betty, who was extremely afraid of the water as a child, but learned how to swim in her fifties. The look on her face when she told me she could now swim is unforgettable. I have another friend who was terrified of public speaking, but conquered that fear when he was older by joining a community group where he could practice his oratory skills with friends. As someone who was very comfortable with detail when I was younger, I now find real wealth in looking at the broader picture, in analysis of things, and in taking time for thinking and contemplation.

Observation of our strengths and weaknesses and calculated practice to build experience in weaker skills leads us to new balance, so we become more like the stork, who stands calmly on one leg in a pool of water and never falls over.

Faith – Xin Yang

Left side: a person	Left side: a person
Right side: word	Right side: two people, one kneeling before the other

We see a person standing by their word in the first character. Questions arise: Is Faith more than a person standing by their words of acceptance of religious doctrine? Because we can recite the words and creeds of our faith, does that mean we have Faith?

The second character Yang, expands the meaning into "to aspire". The two "people" on the right, which almost look like our Roman alphabet letters "CP", are actually ancient representations of one person (C, on the left) facing another person (P, on the right) who is kneeling. We kneel when we revere something. And when we aspire to be like what we revere, transformation is possible.

Faith has often been perceived as having to believe something that you know isn't true, embracing something that is opposite to what your senses tell you about reality. Is *faith* simply another word for *obedience*?

The second character refines our understanding of the conception of faith as God's way of helping us perceive the divine dimension of reality, to revere the divine presence in our lives and the lives of others. Faith involves another way to know the world, another way to look at reality, this time through the lens of the divine dimension, which happens not in the eyes, ears, nose or mouth, through seeing, hearing, smelling or tasting, but instead through the *heart*. The divine dimension of reality is not comprehended through the five sense organs, but is instead recognized through spiritual perception originating in our innermost being.

We also use the word "faith" to talk about things that are not seen. We don't often think about it, but there are many, many things that we cannot perceive, but still have faith in them. Wind. We can't see it, but we know it's there, especially during hurricanes! Love – we know someone loves us, but it we can't "look at" love in the same way that we can look at a flower.

Faith involves mystery – seeing another dimension in reverence. When we open ourselves to that dimension, we can see the divine in everything, from the green of the grass to the sound of children playing.

Faith is not something to grasp, it is a state to grow into.
~ Mohandas Gandhi, advocate and pioneer of nonviolent social protest, leader of India's independence from British colonial rule. 1869-1948

Faith is different from proof; the latter is human, the former is a Gift from God.
~ Blaise Pascal, French mathematician, physicist, and religious philosopher, 1623-1662

Faith is the bird that feels the light when the dawn is still dark.
~ Rabindranath Tagore, Bengali, winner of the 1913 Nobel Prize in Literature, (1861-1901)

The faith that stands on authority is not faith.
~ Ralph Waldo Emerson, American essayist, philosopher, and poet (1803 – 1882)

Harmony – He

Left side: grain ripened on the stalk

Right side: mouth

Some characters are a bit of a mystery. Perhaps this one is painting the picture of having enough to eat in order to live in harmony with your neighbors? What would it take to have a world or even just a neighborhood in harmony?

If we were all alone in the world, just one person, with no one to share anything with, no one to talk to, and no one to eat with, what sort of purpose would we have in the world? When there are "others" we can share love, we can laugh together, and we can also work to overcome the barriers and challenges that come naturally with "more than one" person. Without the other person there is no chance for love, no chance for growth, and no chance for the joy of a lazy morning drinking tea together. Harmony is a real privilege.

The linguists describe Chinese language as being made up of up to 12 main language groups, which are basically mutually unintelligible. I have visited a city in Jiangsu Province which was a tri-corner meeting point of three ancient states. Of the people living in the city, only two of the city gate neighborhoods, the north and east gates, could mutually understand each other. The other two had languages so different that when speaking their dialect, people from the other neighborhoods could not understand what they were saying.

What holds China together? Mandarin, the national language, for one thing. The same characters in the written language are used by everyone in spite of the different dialects for speaking. But the deepest level of harmony comes from the Asian emphasis on group instead of individual, and on relationships instead of tasks.

Having grown up in the United States and been culturally educated in a society that emphasizes the individual, the individual's rights, self-reliance, independence, and individual task focus, I was in great shock when I arrived in China. My "cultural map of reality," my understanding of "what is right" and "what is appropriate" was shaken to its roots.   Spending time in Scotland and Australia had already alerted me to cultural differences, but I had never experienced anything like the differences between China and the West.

During our first year here we were invited to the company's "fall outing." The whole company went, employees, spouses, children – everyone. We piled into a bus, and headed for a small park on the other side of the Yangzi River, and I remember feeling a little overwhelmed with the number of people I was traveling with. We arrived at the tiny park, and proceeded to ramble, several hundred of us, taking in the green trees and the special pond where you could clap your hands and watch the bubbles rise. Everyone exclaimed over this, explaining that the bubbles were like pearls, so therefore this pond was an amazing body of water. What I saw was – a park so crowded with people that I felt crazy. Lots of litter. People bumping into me. Too many people wanting to relate to me. Lots of noise. A rather dirty pond with bubbles. Not much to enjoy from my Western perspective.

How could the company employees be enjoying the outing? They looked positively radiant. What were they seeing that I didn't see? Part of it has to do with harmony. For them, the focus was not so much on the task – the trip to the park – but on the group, on spending time with each other, on having time with families and reveling in the children. On harmony, and creating even deeper levels of harmony. The park was not really important at all.

What would it mean for our spiritual life to focus on harmony in the group instead of the individual? There is no question that all people are connected and intertwined. When we recognize the importance of how much our own happiness depends on the happiness of others, of how greater harmony is possible, then we will have real power to work with.

He who experiences the unity of life sees his own Self in all beings, and all beings in his own Self, and looks on everything with an impartial eye.
~ **Buddha**

I therefore, a prisoner for the Lord, urge you to walk in a manner worthy of the calling to which you have been called, with all humility and gentleness, with patience, bearing with one another in love, eager to maintain the unity of the Spirit in the bond of peace.
~ **Ephesians 4:1-3**

Behold, how good and pleasant it is
        when brothers dwell in unity!
It is like the precious oil on the head,
        running down on the beard,
        on the beard of Aaron,
        running down on the collar of his robes!
~ **Psalm 133:1-2**

The fundamental purpose animating the Faith of God and His Religion is to safeguard the interests and promote the unity of the human race, and to foster the spirit of love and fellowship amongst men.
~ **Baha'i, Tablets of Baha'u'llah**

Be united, speak in harmony,
        let your minds apprehend alike.
Common be your prayer,

    common be the end of your assembly,
Common be your resolutions,
    common be your deliberations.
Alike be your feelings,
    united be your hearts.
Common be your intentions,
    perfect be your unity.
~ **Hinduism, Rig Veda 10.191.2-4**

Dust - Hui

Top left: hand
Bottom: fire

The character for dust is made up of two parts – a hand on the left and fire on the lower right. It is "fire that can be handled."

One year orange yellow dust blew through Beijing on Saint Patrick's Day. What should have been a green day became a brown one. Dust is what happens in the north part of China when there is not enough rain during the year. Nothing, not even planting more trees around the city, makes the dust less if there is a real lack of rain in the Gobi Desert and environs. Hearing about the dust storm brought me back to dust as a spiritual theme of Lent in the Christian tradition.

Lent is the season of dust and ashes. We don't think about dust too much except on Ash Wednesday, when you see the dust smudged on people's foreheads as you walk down the street. Dust used to be a more visible part of spiritual life, as a symbol of remorse for "the things you have done which you wish you hadn't done", the things of spiritual death: anger, jealousy, pride, greed, lying, gossiping and others.

The elements of which we are made, the carbon, oxygen, hydrogen, were all once part of a fiery star. Our bodies incorporate this star-dust, the "fire that can be handled", these elements of life, into our very being. And on top of the physical chemical bricks of which we were born, we also embody the divine spirit, which makes us more than a composite of rock or gasses.

So we are made of "fire that can be handled," and also the divine spirit-fire that is breathed into us at birth, that part of us that knows and understands Love, the sign of God's presence in the dust. Love is what gives us life. It is what will last after the dust is dust again. This prayer from St. Columba of the island of Iona in Scotland, a monk during the Dark Ages in Europe, talks of the flame of love that never ceases. The monasteries he founded were centers of learning, orphanages, and places of hospitality for the people around them. Columba taught by preaching and example and many were touched by his life.

Kindle in our hearts, O God,
The flame of love that never ceases,
That it may burn in us, giving light to others.
May we shine for ever in your temple,
Set on fire with your eternal light,
Even your Son Jesus Christ,
Our savior and redeemer.

~ St. Columba of Iona, Irish missionary monk (521-597)

Smooth, Flowing, Without a Hitch, Obey – Shun

Left side: river

Right side: leaf

The three lines on the left portray a river, with its two banks and stream flowing down the middle. And floating gently on the river is the ancient character for a leaf, portrayed on the right side.

There is incredible gentleness in a leaf that is floating on a stream, flowing with the currents. It is not struggling, fighting, or bemoaning its path. When it flows with the stream, it moves effortlessly with nothing blocking it.

True gentleness is not just being meek or letting oneself be pushed around by circumstances. There is a story about a machine at a factory that could flatten cars, but could also crack a walnut shell and leave the inner meat whole. Gentleness can be a willingness to "go with the flow" and at the same time a truly gentle person can have power under great control. Gandhi had great gentleness in his non-violent stance, and yet had great power as a leader of India's independence movement.

When I consider Jesus' response to the events of Holy Week leading up to his death, it is his gentleness that rests in my mind. Power was swirling around him. He could call for rebellion or revolution or war, but he didn't. Soldiers came to seize him and Jesus told his disciples to stand aside and put down their swords. I have heard the occasional comment that Jesus was foolish to let this happen. The incredible thing was his gentleness.

Take my yoke upon you and learn from me, for I am gentle and humble in heart, and you will find rest for your souls. –
~ Matthew 11:29

Be completely humble and gentle; be patient, bearing with one another in love.
~ Ephesians 4:2

"In a gentle way, you can shake the world."
~ Mohandas Gandhi, advocate and pioneer of nonviolent social protest, leader of India's independence from British colonial rule. 1869-1948

Forgive – Yuan Liang

Outer: cliff	Left side: word
Inner: spring of water	Right side: grand

The first character in the word for forgive has deep meaning.   The interior part means a spring of water which is flowing from a cliff, shown by the character's outer border.   A spring of refreshing water that falls freely from great heights, liquid mercy.

The second character includes "word," a word of forgiveness.   We find this piece in many characters.   The right side means "grand."   Used in the character for the capital of China, it is pronounced "jing" when it appears by itself.   Capitals of a nation are built to look grand, but words of forgiveness are more grand.

The image of water rushing from a cliff brings to mind several aspects of forgiveness. One is that forgiveness requires strength, and is not something that shows weakness.   Another is that water from springs is never-ending, and that is true for our need to forgive – there will always be something.   But the water also brings the image of soothing relief – when we can gather enough strength to forgive, we will experience the "living water" that restores us to real health.

Recently I went to a traditional Chinese doctor for the pain I had from an old injury in my ankle. We got to talking about pain and places in the body when the qi (the electricity of the body, life energy that circulates within us) becomes stuck or blocked. He told me that injuries often rear their heads again one year later, or several years later, as "stuck qi" and pain at that same time of the year. As I thought back, I realized that it was exactly the five year anniversary of my father-in-law's death. He had passed away just after a huge snow storm during which I had re-injured my ankle, and indeed, this year, five years later, there had been a huge snow storm too at that time of year. The injury, sadness, and time of year had been bound up together and reappeared on the same date five years later. He said that psychological injuries can show up as physical pain as well.

We have all been hurt by others (as we have also been the source of hurt for others). We may have to actively forgive someone many times before the deepest hurt has been released. Jesus told his disciples to forgive others seventy-seven times seven, a number that indicates no end. For me this has been very true. I have often had to do the work of forgiveness over and over until I felt truly free of the pain and burden. Forgiveness is deep process that often has to be done over and over in our heart, and after the right amount of time, the work will blossom into real and complete forgiveness.

Hatred never ceases by hatred
But by love alone is healed.
This is the ancient and eternal law.
~ **Buddhism, Dhammapada 6**

If you want to see the heroic,
look at those who can love
in return for hatred.
If you want to see the brave,
look for those who can forgive.
~ **Hinduism. Bhagavad Gita**

Overcome any bitterness that may have come because you were not up to the magnitude of the pain entrusted to you. Like the mother of the world who carries the pain of the world in her heart, you are sharing in a certain measure of that cosmic pain, and are called upon to meet it in joy instead of self-pity.
~ **Pir Vilayat Khan, Sufi tradition**

Forgiveness honors the heart's greatest dignity. Whenever we are lost, it brings us back to the ground of love.
~ **Jack Kornfield, American Buddhist teacher and author**

Then Peter came up and said to him, "Lord, how often will my brother sin against me, and I forgive him? As many as seven times?" Jesus said to him, "I do not say to you seven times, but seventy times seven.
~ **Matthew 18: 21-22**

He who forgives and makes peace, shall find his reward for it from God. Where there is forgiveness, there is God.
~ **Sikhism, Kabir, Vol. 6**

Recompense injury with kindness.
~ **Taoism, Tao Te Ching 63**

Love – Ai

Complicated script: Simplified script

Top three lines (the same for both characters)- breath
reversed or stopped

Middle: heart   _____

Bottom: friend   Bottom: graceful
                                     movement

When I talk to Chinese calligraphers, they often get quite heated about simplified characters.   They don't like them.   The simplification often robs a character of the meaning that calligraphers can see in the multifaceted parts of the complicated form.   An English equivalent might be the words "television" and "TV".   The word television contains the Greek root word *tele*, which means "far off", and a Latin root, *vis*, meaning "to see or look".   The word means something all the way to its roots. TV is devoid of meaning, with no poetry to it.

The character for "love" in Chinese is one that really irritates calligraphers.   The top is the same for both, and has three dots between horizontal lines, which is an ancient character meaning "breath reversed or stopped".

What happens after the wide horizontal stroke in the middle is where the trouble begins! The traditional character (to the left) has a "heart" character plus an ancient character on the bottom which means "graceful movement". It is a poem in graphic form - love breathes life into our hearts, and brings grace to our movements.

I have to admit, simplifying characters has helped thousands of formerly illiterate Chinese become literate by shortening the numbers of strokes necessary to write a character. With fewer strokes, a character is much easier to remember. And so we discover in the simplified form, the character for "friend" below the middle line. Without the heart it is not as poetic as the complicated version but you can see another aspect, that love is "breathing with the love of a friend."

Love is complicated, so I can relate to the calligraphers' point of view. Most important of all, love is one of those things that is both unseen and seen. When we have a warm feeling of love in our hearts, it is unseen. But that warm feeling can manifest in many ways – the hug or kiss, the gift – little or big, different kinds of help, aid, support, encouragement, or the simple gift of time together.

One of the best books in recent years to unravel the thorny question of love is The Five Love Languages of Children (Chapman and Campbell). They spent years researching and analyzing how love is expressed, and summarized their findings in this book. They discovered that love is expressed much like languages, through:

1. Physical touch - hugs, holding hands, pats, kisses.

2. Words - of affirmation, support, encouragement, including "I love you", "Good job" or "Thank you for..."

3. Giving and receiving - not necessarily big presents, but even small things, like a wild flower, or a bar of soap.

4. Acts of service and help - making a cup of tea, fixing something that is broken, helping with a project.

5. Quality time - focusing on someone, spending time with them doing anything at all, not necessarily talking.

The critical thing is that, as with language, most people tend to feel love through only one or two forms, and may not experience some of the others as love at all. It is like speaking French but not German. For example, a person might feel very loved when someone gave them words of support, but feel little or nothing when someone gave them a present. Or vice-versa. So perhaps you may feel like you have someone in your family who has never "really" loved you. It is highly possible that they have "loved" you, but not in the language that you understand as love. When we have grasped this, we have a new kind of freedom to discover how to love someone in the way they will understand, and how to ask for love in ways that we will feel deeply.

Training is needed in order to love properly; and to be able to give happiness and joy, you must practice deep looking directed toward the other person you love. Because if you do not understand this person, you cannot love properly. Understanding is the essence of love. If you cannot understand, you cannot love.
~ Thich Nhat Hanh, Vietnamese Zen Buddhist monk, teacher, author, poet and peace activist, author of *Peace is Every Step*

So we have come to know and to believe the love that God has for us. God is love, and whoever abides in love abides in God, and God abides in him.
~ 1 John 4:16

Like a caring mother
Holding and guarding the life
Of her only child,
So with a boundless heart
Of loving kindness,
Hold yourself and all beings
As your beloved children.
~ Buddha

Love is patient; love is kind; love is not envious or boastful or arrogant or rude. It does not insist on its own way; it is not irritable or resentful; it does not rejoice in wrong-doing, but rejoices in the truth. It bears all things, believes all things, hopes all things, endures all things.

~ **1 Corinthians 13:4-7**

Love is victorious in attack and invulnerable in defense.

~ **Tao Te Ching 67**

Splendid – Hua

A complete picture: The emerging flowers and leaves of a plant. *Hua*, **pronounced Hwah, means Magnificent. Splendid. Glorious.**

There is a story told by Jean Houston, famous author, scholar, and founder of the Foundation for Mind Research. She told how she went to hear a presentation by Helen Keller who was blind and deaf. Houston said she felt she must go speak to her, and offered her face to Helen so she could feel and "see" it. This is what she said of the experience: "She read my whole face and I blurted out: 'Miss Keller, why are you so happy?' and she laughed and laughed, saying: 'My child, it is because I live each day as if it were my last and life, with all its moments, is so full of glory."

Good Friday to Easter Sunday is quite a ride. We roll from deep grief to great joy. Sometimes I have felt it a little overwhelming. But it is true that pain and disappointment are woven together into one fabric with the happiness and pleasure in our lives. Before Easter came Good Friday. Jesus' death was tragic. But understood within the fabric of divine love, the opposites of death and life unite and what is profane becomes sacred again.

Finding peace in life's rolling waves which bring both joy and unhappiness, beauty and ugliness, confusion and clarity, grief and delight, is our daily task. This is spiritual work. Spiritual work is not just something for Sunday, or Easter, or for monks, nuns, or ministers. Our souls grow when we develop a welcoming spirit to salute everything we meet, both pleasurable and disagreeable, painful and joyous, fearful and peaceful, with a respectful and kind heart.   Honoring what IS and respecting the truth is not easy, but is the path to spiritual freedom and peace.   In that is the birth of a deeper level of compassion in our hearts.

If there be anywhere on earth a lover of God who is always kept safe, I know nothing of it, for it was not shown to me. But this was shown: that in falling and rising again we are always kept in that same precious love.
~ **Julian of Norwich, British mystic, (1342-1416)**

This being human is a guest house.
Every morning a new arrival.
A joy, a depression, a meanness,
Some momentary awareness comes
As an unexpected visitor.
Welcome and entertain them all
Even if they're a crowd of sorrows,
Who violently sweep your house
Empty of its furniture.
Still treat each guest honorably,
He may be clearing you out
For some new delight.
The dark thought, the shame, the malice,
Meet them at the door laughing,
And invite them in.
Be grateful for whoever comes,
Because each has been sent
As a guide from beyond.
~ **Rumi, Persian mystic and poet, (1207-1273)**

And as to me, I know of nothing else but miracles.
~ **Walt Whitman, American poet, essayist, journalist, and humanist, author of *Leaves of Grass* (1819-1892)**

Transformation - Bian Hua

Top center: word

Top left and right: threads - this part of the character is used for its phonetic sound, but by picking this particular phonetic some new aspects of the concept are revealed.

Below - To strike

Left: A person

Right: A person, transformed

Transformation requires effort, like the effort used in chopping wood or striking a bell.   Effort, movement, force.

In the early centuries of the church, when huge numbers of people moved out to the desert to live either alone as a solitary hermit or in Christian community, there were famous stories told of some of the leaders of the communities.   These accounts have been gathered together in various collections of stories of the Desert Fathers.   One of my favorites is about Abba Joseph, who encourages one of his followers to move on past rote spiritual practice into a more dynamic spirituality.

Abba Lot came to Abba Joseph and said, "Father, according as I am able, I keep my little rule, and my little fast, my prayer and meditation, and contemplative silence; and according as I am able I strive to cleanse my heart of thoughts. Now what should I do?"

The elder rose up in reply and stretched out his hands to heaven, and his fingers became like ten lamps of fire. He said: "Why not be totally transformed into fire?"

(This was encouraging him to step out of his "little rule" routine where he had limited himself – as the character implies, and begin to use the power of love, understanding, forgiveness, and gratitude to transform his life.)

We have heard the story about Jesus' resurrection each Easter. The spiritual question before us is now about our own. Jesus is already gone from his tomb. He didn't sit there and entertain visitors. He went out and met with his friends. And after he met with his friends, they had huge transformations, becoming stronger, more loving, wiser, and more courageous.

The question now is whether or not we are willing to abandon our own tombs – the ones filled with anxiety, fear, despair, anger, lack of forgiveness, selfishness, and our negative habits and thoughts, and move onto the path set before us, fired by the transforming flames of love, kindness, caring, understanding, forgiveness, and generosity. This is the resurrection energy that we can use to transform ourselves and spread God's joy, love and light out into the world.

Appendix

The Chinese Character Writing System, Copyright © 2009 by Richard W. Bodman. Used with the author's permission.

1. *Chinese script*

The oldest examples of writing are called *jiǎgǔwén*, i.e., inscriptions on "oracle bones" [the plastrons of turtles, or the scapulae of oxen] that date from the Shang dynasty, ca. 1800 BC. These were discovered at Anyang in the 1930s. More recent excavations of Neolithic sites have uncovered pottery with markings that may be writing, which would push back the invention of writing much farther, but this is still controversial. Before China was unified by the Qin empire in 251 BC, the system of writing in characters was not regularized and included lots of local variants. While the Chinese script is not as ancient as Egyptian or Akkadian, it ranks with only a few other scripts that have been continuously used from ancient times to the present.

Let's look at the terms the Chinese themselves came up with. Xu Shen, the author of the preface to one of the earliest Chinese dictionaries, the *Shuo wen jie zi*, [ca. 120 AD] came up with a theory of the "six types of writing" or "六书 liu shu." Of these, the first five are well explained, while the sixth type is still a puzzle for scholars.

1. 象形 xiàngxíng, or "pictogram" [lit., image and form]
2. 指事 zhǐshì, or "ideogram" [lit., pointing to something]
3. 会意 huìyì, or "compound ideograms" [lit., combined meanings]
4. 形声 xíngshēng, or "radical-phonetic compounds" [lit., form and sound]
5. 假借 jiǎjiè, or "phonetic borrowings" [rebuses] [lit., false borrowing]
6. 转注 zhuǎnzhù, or "transformed cognates [?]."

2. Pictograms

Only about six hundred characters fall into the category of pictograms. And only in the earliest stages of the script, in the oracle bone and seal script, are the pictorial elements really recognizable. These, however, are the examples that most people remember. . Examples would be the characters for mountain 山, water 水, tree 木, sun 日 and moon 月. Pictograms are best adapted for representing nouns.

3. Ideograms

There are probably far fewer in the category of "ideogram", a symbol for an idea. These would include the numbers one through three, up and down, center, as well as "root" and "tip of a branch." 一二三上下中本末. These last two are made by taking the character for *mu* 木 "tree" and adding one stroke, either to mark the lower part, or *ben* "root", or the upper part, the *mo* "tip." All the above examples, except the last two, for "root" and "tip" can be found in oracle bone inscriptions.

4. Compound ideograms

These are formed from the combination of two or more symbols: such as:

a. 日+ 月= 明 "sun" and "moon" to make *ming*, "bright"
b. 女+ 子=好"woman" and "son/child" to make *hao*, "good"
c. 木+ 木=林"tree" and "tree" to make *lin*, "forest"

My character set does not allow me to show the symbol for "roof" as a separate character, so I can't break up 家 to show it as the combination of "roof" and "pig", meaning "home" or "family", nor to break up 安 to show it as the combination of "roof" and "woman". Nor do I have the traditional character set, which would allow me to show you the combination of three women as "jian", meaning "adultery."

There are presumably a fair number of characters in the category of "compound ideograms", far more than in the category of simple "ideograms."

All of these examples are found in oracle bone script.

5. Radical-phonetic compounds

The largest category, containing over 90% of modern characters, is the "radical-phonetic" group. These characters are composed of two elements: a "radical" which indicates the category of object into which the word falls, and a "phonetic" which indicates the pronunciation as of about 100 AD. The imperial dictionary compiled by the Kangxi emperor in the late 1600s identified 214 radicals under which all the characters were grouped. There are perhaps 500 or so of the phonetic elements. In this combination of signific and phonetic elements, the Chinese script resembles both Egyptian hieroglyphics and Mayan writing. Let's take the example of the element 加 "jia" [by itself meaning "to add"] which can be used as the phonetic element in characters with different radicals: 笳 with the bamboo radical, in the combination "hujia" 胡笳 meaning "nomad flute"; 架 with the wood radical, meaning "frame" or "rack"; 驾 with the horse radical, meaning "to drive" a carriage or car; and 痂 with the sickness radical to mean "a scab, or crust." All the above are pronounced "jia" in various tones, but it also occurs as 咖 with the mouth radical， pronounced as the "kā" in "kāfēi" or "coffee." Historically, the same phonetic, with different radicals, was used to represent the "kya" or "ka" sound in Sanskrit, as in 释迦牟尼, the transliteration for Skt. *Sakyamuni* [pronounced in modern Chinese as "shijiamouni"]; and as in 袈裟 [modern Chinese jiāshā] for Skt. *kasaya*, a patchwork outer vestment worn by a Buddhist monk.

The *Shuo Wen Jie Zi* is a dictionary of seal script characters, the descendants of oracle bone script. The seal script shows plenty of examples of radical phonetic compounds.

6. Phonetic loans, or "rebus" characters.

We can write simple English sentences with rebuses, i.e. a drawing of an eye plus a drawing of a saw plus the capital letter U generates the sentence "I saw you." Here the rebus characters are used for their sound alone, not for their meanings. In text messaging, people use "4" to represent "for" and "8" to represent "ate." These would also be examples of rebuses. The word "xi" 西 originally meant "to roost" but was later borrowed to represent the homophone meaning "west." The word "qiu" 求 originally meant a fur or pelt but was later borrowed to represent the homophone meaning "to seek." The word "xu" 须 originally meant a beard but was later borrowed to represent the homophone meaning "must."

7. Transformed cognates

There is some debate over the meaning of this category. The two standard examples are the words "kao"考 and "lao 老" which are related both in shape and meaning; their pronunciation in archaic Chinese may also be close. "Kao" refers to a deceased ancestor, while "lao" means old. [A third example might be the word "xiao" for "filial piety", the required service the young owe towards their elders and ancestors.]

8. Number of characters needed for literacy.

The largest Chinese dictionary contains close to 40,000 characters, but many of these are alternate forms or archaic usages. The average educated user needs between two to three thousand characters for reading a newspaper or magazine. At my college, our new text introduces 418 characters in the first year, but because individual characters can combine to make polysyllabic words, a far larger vocabulary can be created from them.

Literacy takes a longer time to acquire in Chinese than in many other languages. The Chinese elementary school student acquires the necessary vocabulary to read and write in six years. These students typically have several hours of homework per night. In the past, rote memory was the primary method for inculcating literacy, and it probably still is today. Before the 20th century, pupils would learn to recite the Chinese classics and classical poetry often without understanding what they were saying.

9. Traditional versus simplified characters

Because the task of becoming literate in Chinese is considerable, the current mainland government, beginning in the 1950s, started to simplify the written script, reducing the number of strokes needed to write individual characters. The simplified characters are called *jiantizi*. Literacy has increased considerably, though in some rural areas only lower primary schools are available, up to grade three.

Chinese living in Hong Kong, Macao and Taiwan, as well as overseas Chinese continue to use the traditional characters, or *fantizi*. The foreign learner of Chinese should ideally know both traditional and simplified characters.

Here are sample characters in traditional and simplified forms:

Traditional	Simplified	Transliteration	Meaning
聽	听	Tīng	to listen
說	说	Shūo	to speak
讀	读	Dú	to read
寫	写	Xǐe	to write
書	书	Shū	book
筆	笔	Bǐ	pen, brush

The simplified characters clearly use fewer strokes. In "shuo" [to speak], the simplified character has only simplified the left-hand element, which is the "speech" radical. Most of the other examples, however, are changed significantly. For example, the traditional forms of the characters for "shū" [book] and "bǐ" [pen, brush] show that they share a common element, which disappears in the simplified versions.

10. **Pros and cons of a character-based script**

Precisely because the Chinese writing system is not phonetic, people from all over China can read it in their local pronunciation. And for the same reason, people with some education can read documents in classical Chinese dating from the time of Confucius, ca. 500 B.C. The script has thus served as a powerful unifying force in Chinese politics, as well as a means for keeping Chinese in touch with their past.

But since the Chinese script takes so long to learn, why not abandon it and just use pīnyīn (abcs)? I can imagine two sorts of objections, one technical and one cultural.

First, even though pǔtōnghuà is much more widely spoken and understood than it was fifty years ago, there are still many people who cannot spell pīnyīn accurately, including a large number of people who speak sub-dialects of Mandarin. Second, abandoning Chinese characters would be equivalent to abandoning three millennia of Chinese written culture. The Chinese classics transcribed into pinyin would be incomprehensible, because there would be too many homophones. Further, Chinese have a strong emotional and psychological attachment to their written language. It's a symbol of their identity and something that makes them unique.

If China were to employ a latin-based script for the Chinese language of today, it would conceivably work, though it would be extra work for all those who don't speak standard Mandarin. But if China's classical literature were translated into a latin-based script, it would result in meaningless nonsense. Why? Classical Chinese and modern Chinese are related but quite different languages, as far apart as Anglo-Saxon and English, or Latin and Romanian. There have been considerable changes in phonology, grammar, vocabulary, etc in the 2500 years since the heyday of classical Chinese. A few modern scholars, both Chinese and Western, have reconstructed the sounds of ancient and archaic Chinese, but modern readers of classical Chinese approach it through the medium of written characters and not a phonetic script. While the sounds have changed, the meanings of the written characters are much more stable. But if ancient texts were transcribed into modern pronunciation in a latin script, the modern reader would now lose the visual clue. Moreover, many words that once possessed distinct sounds in classical Chinese have become homophones in modern pronunciation.

Here is a saying from Confucius, for example, with pronunciations in archaic Chinese and modern Chinese, as given by Bernhard Karlgren in his book, *The Chinese Language*, New York, The Ronald Press, 1949, p. 21:

子曰：我未见 好仁者恶不仁者。
Tsig giwăt ngâ miwd kian xôg niěn tia âg pwt niěn tia [reconstructed archaic Chinese]
Zi yue: wo wei jian hao ren zhe wu bu ren zhe [modern Chinese]
Master says: I not see love good one-who hate not good one-who [English, word by word]

The Master said: "I have never yet seen somebody who (really) loves good and hates evil."

One of the big differences you will notice is that the reconstructed archaic Chinese has a wealth of syllable-final consonants which modern Chinese lacks.

Students learning Chinese as a foreign language also struggle with the problem of homophones. At the level of the syllable, many individual sounds can be represented by a variety of different characters, each representing a different meaning. In the archaic language, most of these characters would have had distinct readings, but the process of linguistic change over centuries has stripped many of the original final consonants from syllables, and caused other changes as well.

For instance, the sound "xin" in modern Chinese potentially represents either of the following:

心 *siəm, meaning "heart" or "mind"

新　*siĕn, meaning "new"

This illustrates the fact that all syllables in archaic Chinese ending in -m have changed to -n in modern Chinese.

The sound "xue" in modern Chinese may represent:
雪　*siwat, meaning "snow" or
学　*g'ôk, meaning "to study, learn"

This shows an even greater diversity, in both initials and finals, in the archaic forms. The archaic reconstructions I have quoted come from Bernhard Karlgren, *Grammata Serica Recensa*, Stockholm: Museum of Far Eastern Antiquities, 1964. These reconstructed pronunciations are now somewhat outdated in terms of contemporary scholarship, but as far as I know there is no dictionary other than Karlgren's.

Of course, while English spelling is phonetic, it is still not easy, and is far less systematized than say Spanish. If all English homophones were spelled identically, then we'd lose the distinctions between "sum" and "some", "one" and "won"; the metal "lead" and the past tense of the verb "to lead", i.e. "led"; "blue" and "blew"; "knew" and "new"; "write" "right" and "wright"; "borough" "burrow" and "burro"; "insight" and "incite"; and possibly "Virgin" and "version." If these distinctions were lost, we'd lose some clues to the history and etymology of English, but we could still read our modern language. If the Chinese adopted phonetic spelling, they could still read their modern language, but the classical language would be lost in a cloud of homophones.

Additionally, China's writing system is a potent symbol of identity; it's something that sets Chinese apart from foreigners and gives them a sense of uniqueness. That's not to say that some cultures haven't changed their scripts, but they have all arguably paid a price for it. Thus, Egyptians exchanged hieroglyphic and demotic script for Arabic; Vietnamese gave up Chinese script and their own Nom script in exchange for a Latin script; and Kemal Attaturk reformed the Turkish language and grammar, replacing an Arabic script with a Latin script. In doing so, these peoples all lost access to their past history and literature.

Works Cited

Augustine, S. (n.d.). *St. Augustine Quotes*. Retrieved June 29, 2009, from ThinkExist.com: http://en.thinkexist.com/quotation/god-is-not-what-you-imagine-or-what-you-think-you/697103.html

Bahá'u'lláh. (n.d.). *Tablets of Bahá'u'lláh Revealed After the Kitáb-i-Aqdas*. Retrieved 7 4, 2009, from Bahai Reference Library: http://reference.bahai.org/en/

Bai, L. (n.d.). *Tang Shi - 300 Tang Poems*. Retrieved June 29, 2009, from Wen Gu - Chinese Classics and Translatins: http://afpc.asso.fr/wengu/wg/wengu.php?m=NOzh&l=Tangshi&no=55

Barks, C. (1995). *The Essential Rumim - reissue*. New York: HarperCollins Publishers, Inc.

Bing, X. (n.d.). *Infinite Stars*. Retrieved from Binxin Academy: http://www.bingxin.org/databank/news/2003/16/new_page_2.htm

Bonder, R. N. (1999). *Yiddishe Kop*. Boston: Shambhala Publications Inc.

Buddha. (n.d.). *Celebrations*. Retrieved 7 5, 2009, from Jubilee Community: http://www.jubileecommunity.org/bulletins/2008/3_16_08.pdf

Buddha. (n.d.). *Dhammapada*. Retrieved 7 4, 2009, from The Big View - About Buddhism: http://www.thebigview.com/buddhism/dhammapada.html

Buddha. (n.d.). *Prayers*. Retrieved 6 29, 2009, from Twelve Beads: http://www.twelvebeads.com/Prayers.html

Buddha Quotes. (n.d.). Retrieved 7 4, 2009, from ThinkExist: http://thinkexist.com/quotation/he_who_experiences_the_unity_of_life_sees_his_own/200715.html

Burke, N., & Nassal, J. (1998). *How to Pray*. Deerfield Beach: Health Communications, Inc.

Cheng-chueh, Zhengjue, & Taigen, D. L. (2000). *Cultivating the empty field: the silent illumination of Zen Master*. Boston: Tuttle Publishing.

Chesterton, G. K. (n.d.). *Orthodoxy (1908)*. Retrieved 6 29, 2009, from Leadership U: http://www.leaderu.com/cyber/books/orthodoxy/orthodoxy.html

Chodron, P. (1997). *When Things Fall Apart*. Boston: Shambhala.

Confucius, 5.-4. B. (1996). *Confucius, The Analects*. Retrieved June 29, 2009, from Chinese Philosophy: http://www.wsu.edu/~dee/CHPHIL/ANALECTS.HTM

Conroy, S. (2003). *Mother Teresa's Lessons of Love & Secrets of Sanctity*. Huntington, IN: Our Sunday Visitor, Inc.

Einstein, A. (n.d.). *Albert Einstein quotes*. Retrieved 6 29, 2009, from ThinkExist: http://thinkexist.com/quotation/everything_should_be_made_as_simple_as_possible/10113.html

Einstein, A. (n.d.). *Albert Einstein Quotes*. Retrieved 6 29, 2009, from On Truth & Reality: http://www.spaceandmotion.com/Albert-Einstein-Quotes.htm

Einstein, A. (1931). The World As I See It. In A. Einstein, *Living Philosophies* (pp. 193-194). New York: Simon Schuster.

Einstein, A., & Russell, B. (1955, July 9). *The Russell-Einstein Manifesto*. Retrieved June 29, 2009, from Pugwash Online: http://www.pugwash.org/about/manifesto.htm

Emerson, R. W. (1803-1882). *Ralph Waldo Emerson Quotes*. Retrieved June 29, 2009, from Quotes.net: "Ralph Waldo Emerson." Quotes.net. STANDS4 LLC, 2009. 28 June. 2009. http://www.quotes.net/quote/501

Emmons, R. A., & Hill, J. (2001). *Words of Gratitude for Mind, Body, and Soul*. Templeton Foundation Press.

Farhardi, A. G. (1996). *Anasari of Heart (1006-1089)*. Surrey: RoutledgeCurzon.

Gandhi, M. (n.d.). *Mahatama Gandhi*. Retrieved 7 4, 2009, from QuotationsBook: http://quotationsbook.com/quote/13953/

Gita, T. B. (n.d.). *The Bhagavad Gita*. Retrieved 7 4, 2009, from Exploring Ancient World Cultures - Readings from Ancient India: http://eawc.evansville.edu/anthology/gita.htm

Grigg, R. (1993). *The New Lao Tzu: A Contemporary Tao Te Ching*. Rutland, Vermont and Tokyo, Japan: Charles E. Tuttle Co., Inc.

Hammarskjöld, D. (1964). *Markings*. Alfred A. Knopf.

Hanh, T. N. (1997). *True Love: A Practice for Awakening the Heart*. Boston: Shambhala Publications, Inc.

Hogan, L. (1995). *Dwellings*. New York: Simon & Schuster.

Ikkyu. (n.d.). *Ikkyu and the Crazy Cloud Anthology*. Retrieved June 29, 2009, from Panhala: http://www.panhala.net/Archive/Love_Letters.html

Ikkyu. (n.d.). *Reflections on Ikkyu*. Retrieved June 29, 2009, from Empty Sky Vipassana Sangha: http://www.emptyskysangha.org/ikkyu.htm

Jones, N. (1995). *Power of Raven Wisdom of Serpent: Celtic Women's Spirituality*. Lindisfarne Press.

Khan, P. V. (n.d.). *Reconnecting Wi*. Retrieved 7 4, 2009, from Ashokah Life: http://www.ashokaedu.net/coursesM/34/ecologyjm5.htm

Kornfield, J. (2000). *After the Ecstasy, the Laundry: How the Heart Grows Wise on the Spiritual Path*. New York: Bantam.

Kornfield, J. (2002). *The Art of Forgiveness, Lovingkindness, and Peace*. New York: Bantam Books.

Lama, D. (n.d.). *Dalai Lama quotes*. Retrieved 6 29, 2009, from ThinkExist: http://thinkexist.com/quotation/my_religion_is_very_simple-my_religion_is/145384.html

Lao, Z. (n.d.). *Lao Tzu*. Retrieved 6 29, 2009, from Quotes Daddy: http://www.quotesdaddy.com/author/Lao+Tzu/6

L'Engle, M. (1996). *Glimpses of Grace: Daily Thoughts and Reflections*. New York: HarperCollins Publishers.

Lewis, C. S. (1942). *The Screwtape Letters*. New York: HarperCollins Publishers, Inc.

Mathieu, W. A. (1994). *The Musical Life*. Boston: Shambhala.

Merton, T. (1956). *Thoughts in Solitude*. New York: Farrar, Straus and Giroux.

Norwich, J. o. (n.d.). *Julian of Norwich*. Retrieved 7 5, 2009, from Amoira: http://koti.mbnet.fi/amoira/women/julian1.htm

Nouwen, H. (1997). *Bread for the Journey*. New York: HarperCollins Publisher, Inc.

Nouwen, H. (1992). *Life of the Beloved*. New York: The Crossroad Publishing Co.

O'Rourke, P. J. (n.d.). *P. J. O'Rourke quotes*. Retrieved 6 29, 2009, from Brainy Quote: http://www.brainyquote.com/quotes/quotes/p/pjorour104047.html

Pascal, B. (n.d.). *Blaise Pascal Quotes*. Retrieved 7 4, 2009, from ThinkExist: http://thinkexist.com/quotation/faith_is_different_from_proof-the_latter_is_human/12931.html

Roosevelt, F. D. (n.d.). *FDR's First Inaugural Address*. Retrieved 6 29, 2009, from History Matters: http://historymatters.gmu.edu/d/5057/

Rumi. (n.d.). *Mevlana Rumi*. Retrieved 6 29, 2009, from Quotiki: http://www.quotiki.com/people/Mevlana-Rumi/quotes

Rumi. (n.d.). *Poems by Rumi*. Retrieved June 29, 2009, from Greece -Thracian Minorities: http://www.armory.com/~thrace/sufi/poems.html#We are as the flute

Rumi. (n.d.). *Quotes by Rumi*. Retrieved June 29, 2009, from Self-help Healing Arts Journal: http://www.self-help-healing-arts-journal.com/quotes-by-rumi.html

Schweitzer, A. (n.d.). *Kindness Quotes*. Retrieved 6 29, 2009, from Tentmaker Quotes: http://www.tentmaker.org/Quotes/kindnessquotes.htm

Singh, H. R. *Sri Guru Granth Sahib discovered*.

Sri Granth. (n.d.). Retrieved 7 5, 2009, from Sri Granth: http://www.srigranth.org/servlet/gurbani.gurbani?S=y

St. Francis De Sales. (n.d.). Retrieved 7 4, 2009, from Doctors of the Catholic Church: http://www.doctorsofthecatholicchurch.com/F.html

Tagore, R. (1916). *Stray Birds*. New York: The Macmillian Co.

T'ai-Shang Kan-Ying P'ien. (n.d.). Retrieved 7 5, 2009, from Terebess Asia Online (TAO): http://www.terebess.hu/english/taishang.html

Teresa, M., & Tutu, D. (2007). *Love: The Words and Inspiration of Mother Teresa.* Blue Mountain Arts, Inc.

The Bible (NIV). (1984). *The New International Version of the Bible.* Zondervan.

The Golden Rule. (n.d.). Retrieved 6 29, 2009, from Baha'i Community of Oliver Paipoonge: http://www.bahaiop.org/Golden_Rule.html

The Qur'an. (n.d.). Retrieved 7 5, 2009, from USC Center for Jewish-Muslim Engagement: http://www.usc.edu/schools/college/crcc/engagement/resources/texts/muslim/quran/

The Upanishads, Part 2 (SBE15), by Max Müller. (n.d.). Retrieved 6 29, 2009, from Sacred Texts: http://www.sacred-texts.com/hin/sbe15/sbe15105.htm

Thoreau, H. D. (n.d.). *Henry David Thoreau quotes.* Retrieved 6 29, 2009, from ThinkExist: http://thinkexist.com/quotation/as_you_simplify_your_life-the_laws_of_the/208294.html

To Live the Life. (n.d.). Retrieved 7 4, 2009, from http://www.rt66.com/~kjherman/5To_Live_The_Life.htm

Twain, M. (n.d.). *Mark Twain quotes.* Retrieved 6 29, 2009, from ThinkExist: http://thinkexist.com/quotation/kindness_is_a_language_which_the_deaf_can_hear/164698.html

Tzu, L. (1995, 7 29). *Tao Te Ching.* Retrieved 6 29, 2009, from CUNY: http://acc6.its.brooklyn.cuny.edu/~phalsall/texts/taote-v3.html

Unity and Community, World Scripture. (n.d.). Retrieved 7 4, 209, from textfiles.com: http://www.textfiles.com/occult/WORLDSCRIPTURE/theme029.out

Voltaire. *Treatise on Tolerance (1763).*

Voltaire, F. (2008). *Voltaire S Philosophical Dictionary.* BiblioBazaar, LLC.

Wang, J. (1989). The Complete Ci-poems of Li Qingzhao. *Sino-Platonic Papers* .

Whitman, W. (1897). *Plain Label Books - Leaves of Grass.* Retrieved 7 5, 2009, from Google Books: http://books.google.com/books?id=bsw3FiOIY3wC&dq=leaves+of+grass&printsec=frontcover&source=bl&ots=LSIIOzBYMC&sig=sQRxAF1tBHy-Bu8f5nPNOKP91-Q&hl=en&ei=pmBQSoStIJXs6AObuNTaCg&sa=X&oi=book_result&ct=result&resnum=5

Made in the USA
Lexington, KY
22 November 2011